Paws and Icons

Paws and Icons

The Cultural Impact of Famous Cats

Solomon Raj

UNIEK ENTERPRISES

CONTENTS

INDEX

INTRODUCTION

In the huge embroidery of mankind's set of experiences and culture, there exists a special string woven by the captivating and cryptic animals known as felines. Loved for their free spirits, secretive disposition, and perky shenanigans, felines have flawlessly coordinated themselves into the texture of social orders across the globe. Nonetheless, past the customary cat buddies that murmur in our homes, there exists a subset of felines that have risen above the limits of simple pets, accomplishing a notorious status that has made a permanent imprint on our social cognizance.

"Paws and Symbols: The Social Effect of Well known Felines" is an investigation into the unprecedented stories of cat big names whose presence has resounded a long ways past the domains of terraces and lounges. From the sacrosanct felines of old Egypt to the web impressions of the advanced age, this far reaching assessment looks to disentangle the heap manners by which these four-legged associates have molded and affected human culture.

The Authentic Love for Cat Grandness

To grasp the significant effect of well known felines on our social scene, it is basic to dig into the chronicles of history where felines were not just trained partners but rather loved gods. Antiquated Egyptians, specifically, held felines in the most noteworthy regard, adoring them as images of effortlessness and security. Bastet, the catlike goddess, was a demonstration of the worship gave to these animals. As we venture through time, we witness how felines, with their great balance and puzzling charm, became images of heavenly association and guardianship, making a permanent imprint on the workmanship, folklore, and otherworldliness of old civic establishments.

From Catwalks to Feline Recordings: The Ascent of Current Cat Famous people

As mankind progressed from old civilizations to the advanced time, the job of felines developed from sacrosanct creatures to adored partners and, in the end, web sensations. The coming of web-based entertainment stages delivered another period of cat superstar, where common felines became exceptional stars with worldwide fanbases. Testy Feline, Lil Buddy, and Nyan Feline are only a couple of instances of how the web slung these apparently standard pets into the spotlight, making a peculiarity that obscured the lines among virtual and unmistakable notoriety.

Cat Forces to be reckoned with: Felines as Problem solvers

Past the domains of diversion and style, well known felines have become unintentional powerhouses, involving their fame as a stage to resolve basic issues and supporter for change.

From Morris the Feline's job in elevating pet reception to the notorious 'Console Feline' bringing issues to light about protected innovation privileges, these catlike powerhouses are something beyond delightful appearances on screens; they are impetuses for social change and ministers for significant causes.

The Feline's Whimper in Mainstream society

The impact of well known felines reaches out past the computerized domain, invading the universe of writing, workmanship, and mainstream society. From the devilish Cheshire Feline in Lewis Carroll's "Alice's Undertakings in Wonderland" to the notorious animation couple Tom and Jerry, felines have imbued themselves as repeating images and characters, enhancing the social woven artwork with their complex personas. This segment of our investigation expects to analyze the manners by which renowned felines have invaded and molded different types of creative articulation.

The Eventual fate of Cat Distinction: A Continuum of Social Effect

As we leave on this excursion through the social effect of popular felines, contemplating the future direction of cat fame is fundamental. Will the following viral sensation rise up out of the profundities of the web, or will customary media keep on highlighting unprecedented felines? How might the advancing elements of human-creature connections shape the account of popular cats in the years to come? These inquiries highlight the powerful idea of our relationship with felines and the interminable impact they apply on our social account.

In "Paws and Symbols: The Social Effect of Renowned Felines," we welcome you to go with us on an investigation of the enrapturing stories, startling impacts, and getting through traditions of these unprecedented cat figures. Through the parts that follow, we will unwind the complex strings that interface us to these notable felines, following their pawprints across the immense material of human culture.

1. **The Phenomenon of Famous Cats in Modern Culture**

   In the consistently advancing scene of current culture, one specific peculiarity has ascended to noticeable quality, enthralling hearts and rising above the computerized domain - the ascent of popular felines. From the beginning of the web to the present, these catlike big names have become pets as well as social symbols, making a permanent imprint on the shared perspective of society. This investigation dives into the complexities of the peculiarity, following its foundations, grasping its elements, and analyzing the significant effect these well known felines have had on our contemporary social scene.

The Computerized First light: From Viral Sensations to Web Sovereignty
The peculiarity of renowned felines in present day culture tracks down its underlying foundations in the appearance of the web. The computerized age carried with it a democratization of notoriety, permitting normal felines to enthrall crowds internationally through the force of viral substance. Stages like YouTube, Instagram, and TikTok became virtual stages where felines could feature their one of a kind characters, idiosyncrasies, and obvious appeal.

Testy Feline, seemingly one of the earliest web sensations, arose as the trailblazer of this peculiarity. Tardar Sauce, as she was formally known, turned into a short-term big name thanks to her ceaselessly surly articulation. The picture of her unhappy face spread like quickly across web-based entertainment, prompting a huge number of images, product, and, surprisingly, a component film. Cantankerous Feline's ascent denoted the start of another period where felines, paying little heed to raise or foundation, could catch the web's consideration and rise to advanced fame.

Continuing in Crotchety Feline's pawprints, a rush of cat powerhouses surfaced, each with its own exceptional allure. Lil Pal, with her unmistakable appearance because of hereditary oddities, turned into a promoter for unique necessities pets and caught the hearts of millions. Console Feline, an exemplary illustration of feline as-performer, engaged crowds worldwide and even turned into an image in copyright conversations.

The Web-based Entertainment Jungle gym: Felines as Happy Makers
As web-based entertainment developed, renowned felines started to collect devotees as well as effectively draw in with their crowd, transforming their web-based presence into a type of computerized narrating. Stages like Instagram, specifically, turned into a jungle gym for feline powerhouses, offering a visual banquet of delightful previews, clever inscriptions, and frequently diverting jokes.

Feline proprietors changed into content makers, arranging painstakingly created stories around their catlike partners. The charm of these records lies in the cute visuals as well as in the production of appealing and frequently funny personas for the felines. Whether it's a modern feline tasting tea or a wicked one causing problems, these stories have raised felines from simple pets to characters in a continuous computerized adventure.

Besides, virtual entertainment has empowered a feeling of local area among feline fans. Hashtags like #CatsofInstagram and #Caturday have become virtual social occasion spots where individuals share their adoration for cats, cultivating a feeling of association and kinship. In this computerized age, popular felines act as representatives of bliss, giving a genuinely necessary rest from the difficulties of regular day to day existence.

Cat VIPs: Past the Screen and Into the Standard
The effect of well known felines isn't restricted to the computerized domain;

it has poured out over into standard culture. These catlike famous people have risen above their virtual limits, penetrating customary media, publicizing, and even design. The compellingly naturally attractive nature of felines has gone with them well known decisions for brand organizations and publicizing efforts. Take, for instance, the coordinated effort between Choupette, Karl Lagerfeld's spoiled feline, and extravagance brands. Choupette, with her own Instagram account and a way of life befitting a style symbol, turned into the essence of specific design and excellence crusades. This crossing point of high style and cat acclaim exhibits how renowned felines have flawlessly incorporated into the echelons of mainstream society.

Moreover, media outlets has perceived the capability of well known felines to draw in crowds. Feline driven motion pictures, Programs, and narratives have become staples, displaying the existences of these catlike stars. The ubiquity of movies like "Keanu" and narratives like "Kedi" features the getting through interest society has with felines and their assorted characters.

Catvertising: From Viral Recordings to Brand Ministers

In the serious universe of publicizing, the appeal of well known felines has shown to be a strong device. Brands, anxious to take advantage of the enormous internet based crowds these felines order, have enrolled them as ministers for different items and administrations. The intrinsic capacity of felines to bring out sure feelings makes them ideal for promoting efforts, and sponsors have utilized this to make significant and shareable substance.

One of the most striking models is the coordination of felines into business notices. Brands like Friskies, with their "Dear Little cat" series, have excelled at making charming and silly feline driven content that resounds with crowds. These missions advance items as well as benefit from the profound association individuals have with felines, transforming them into successful brand representatives.

From Images to Product: The Business Feline astrophe

The business outcome of well known felines stretches out past commercials into the domain of product. The web's relationship with feline images has converted into a flourishing business sector for feline themed items. From dress and accomplices to home style and writing material, the countenances and shenanigans of renowned felines have tracked down their direction onto a variety of buyer merchandise.

The capacity of these catlike superstars to motivate industrialism is a demonstration of the profound close to home bonds individuals structure with them.

The acquisition of feline product turns into an unmistakable articulation of profound respect and love, permitting fans to integrate their number one cat characters into their day to day routines.

Felines with a Reason: Social Effect and Backing

Past the domain of amusement and commercialization, well known felines have arisen as unforeseen supporters for social causes. Utilizing their boundless allure, these catlike powerhouses utilize their foundation to bring issues to light about issues going from creature government assistance and reception to natural protection.

Irritable Feline, for example, turned into an envoy for the significance of fixing and fixing pets. Lil Pal, with her novel appearance coming about because of hereditary oddities, turned into a promoter for unique necessities creatures, advancing acknowledgment and understanding. The capacity of these felines to rouse positive activity exhibits the compelling job they play in forming public discernments and values.

Felines as Treatment: Profound Effect on Human Prosperity

The peculiarity of renowned felines reaches out past amusement and promotion; it has helpful ramifications for human prosperity. The web is overwhelmed with accounts of individuals tracking down comfort and solace in the virtual friendship of renowned felines. Whether it's a brief video of a fun loving cat or the quieting presence of a feline powerhouse's everyday posts, these computerized communications significantly affect emotional well-being.

Research has recommended that watching feline recordings can prompt superior state of mind and decreased feelings of anxiety. The restorative advantages of the peculiarity reach out past the virtual world, as some treatment creatures are popular felines themselves, offering profound help to those out of luck. The capacity of felines to bring out sure feelings and give a feeling of association highlights their importance in advancing mental and profound prosperity.

The Clouded Side of Cat Notoriety: Abuse and Morals

While the peculiarity of popular felines gives pleasure and diversion to millions, it likewise brings up moral issues about the abuse of these creatures for human entertainment and benefit. The line between certified friendship and commodification becomes obscured as felines are pushed into the spotlight, frequently exposed to the tensions of notoriety without their comprehension or assent.

Issues, for example, the prosperity of felines even with consistent public examination, the obligation of proprietors to focus on their pets' necessities over distinction, and the possible adverse consequence of commercialization on cat government assistance come to the front.

The clouded side of cat distinction prompts an essential discussion about the moral contemplations encompassing the convergence of felines and VIP culture.

The Eventual fate of Renowned Cats: Patterns and Changes

As we explore the ongoing scene of popular felines in current culture, conjecturing on the direction of this phenomenon is fundamental. Will the charm of cat forces to be reckoned with keep on dazzling crowds, or would we say we are near the very edge of another period in which other creature sidekicks become the overwhelming focus? The developing elements of online entertainment, innovation, and cultural qualities will without a doubt shape the eventual fate of popular felines, suggesting charming conversation starters about the life span and supportability of this social peculiarity.

2. **The Rise of Internet Cat Celebrities**

In the huge territory of the web, where images become famous online in a moment and patterns clear across mainlands, a one of a kind and persevering through peculiarity has arisen — the ascent of web feline big names. These catlike powerhouses, with their enchanting shenanigans and unmistakable characters, have caught the hearts of millions as well as reshaped the scene of online culture. This investigation dives into the enrapturing excursion of web feline big names, following their beginnings, analyzing the elements that add to their prominence, and considering the persevering through allure of these computerized cat sensations.

Starting points of the Catlike Web Takeover

The beginning of the web were set apart by an unconstrained ejection of feline related content. As stages like YouTube acquired prominence, clients started sharing recordings of their fuzzy partners participated in charming or entertaining exercises. The web turned into a virtual jungle gym where feline proprietors exhibited the lovable, eccentric, and frequently unforeseen way of behaving of their catlike companions.

One of the trailblazers in this computerized cat transformation was the famous "Console Feline." Starting as an image in 2007, the video highlighted a feline named Fatso playing a console in a way that proposed it was adding to a melodic presentation. The clasp immediately turned into a web sensation, making ready for another period of feline driven content.

The Impetus: Images, Virality, and Worldwide Popularity

The climb of web feline VIPs can be ascribed to the remarkable manner by which feline related content fits virality. Felines have an inborn capacity to inspire a scope of feelings, from sheer joy to wild giggling. Web clients, looking for a break from the ordinary, tracked down comfort and diversion in the unusual universe of felines.

Images assumed a critical part in catapulting felines into the computerized spotlight. Whether it was the indifferent appearance of Crotchety Feline, the bold endeavors of "Nyan Feline," or the sensational "Emotional Chipmunk" style of the "Shocked Pikachu" feline, these images became social standards that rose above geological and semantic limits. The general allure of feline images added to the fast dispersal of cat content, transforming normal felines into exceptional web-based characters.

The Crotchety Feline Peculiarity

No investigation of web feline famous people is finished without diving into the peculiarity that is Surly Feline. Tardar Sauce, the feline behind the notable scowling face, turned into a worldwide sensation after a photograph was posted on Reddit in 2012. The picture turned into a web sensation, and Testy Feline immediately turned into an image of web culture.

What put Surly Feline aside was her never-endingly cantankerous articulation as well as the smart inscriptions that went with her pictures. The subtitles, composed according to the viewpoint of a harsh and skeptical feline, resounded with crowds, prompting far and wide acknowledgment and, surprisingly, a line of product. Testy Feline's impact stretched out past the computerized domain, with appearances on TV programs, in books, and, surprisingly, a wax sculpture at Madame Tussauds.

The Progress to Virtual Entertainment Fame

As virtual entertainment stages multiplied, web feline big names tracked down another stage to feature their appeal and magnetism. Instagram, specifically, turned into a sanctuary for feline powerhouses, giving an outwardly engaging stage to sharing previews of their delightful lives. Accounts devoted to renowned felines amassed devotees in the large numbers, making a committed local area of cat fans.

Accounts like that of Lil Pal, with her particular appearance because of hereditary peculiarities, earned consideration for her extraordinary highlights as well as for the certifiable association her proprietor encouraged with the crowd. Lil Buddy's excursion, recorded through Instagram posts and a YouTube series, exhibited the cozy and interesting parts of existence with a unique necessities feline, further setting the connection between web felines and their worldwide fanbases.

From Amusement to Support

The ascent of web feline famous people rose above the domain of diversion, developing into a stage for support and social effect. Felines like Lil Buddy and Testy Feline utilized their popularity to bring issues to light about significant causes. Testy Feline, for instance, turned into a backer for fixing and fixing pets, resolving the issue of pet overpopulation.

The span and impact of these catlike powerhouses permitted them to become envoys for different worthy missions. Whether it was advancing reception, raising assets for creature government assistance associations, or pushing for exceptional requirements pets, web feline VIPs showed the potential for positive change that could come from their computerized fame.

The Commercialization of Cat Distinction

With distinction came business potential open doors for web feline VIPs. Brands perceived the advertising capability of these catlike powerhouses and started working together with them for limited time crusades. From feline driven product to organizations with pet food marks, the commercialization of cat distinction turned into a worthwhile road for both feline proprietors and brands hoping to take advantage of the tremendous crowd these web superstars directed.

Choupette, the spoiled feline of style originator Karl Lagerfeld, embodies the crossing point of cat notoriety and top of the line marking. Choupette's way of life, recorded on her Instagram account, displayed a universe of extravagance and fabulousness, making her a fitting teammate for design and magnificence crusades. The converging of cat impact with very good quality marking denoted another wilderness in the commercialization of web feline big names.

Felines as Advanced Content Makers

Web feline famous people aren't simply detached subjects of content; they've become computerized content makers by their own doing. Proprietors, perceiving the allure of their felines, started organizing content that exhibited the novel characters of their catlike buddies. Whether it was making clever subtitles, making drawing in stories, or partaking in moving difficulties, these felines became dynamic members in the substance creation process.

Stages like TikTok, with its short-structure video design, gave another road to feline powerhouses to feature their appeal. Felines partaking in difficulties, showing their dexterity, or essentially captivating in energetic conduct wound up at the very front of viral patterns. The capacity of felines to consistently adjust to the developing scene of computerized content creation built up their status as persevering through web superstars.

The Clouded Side of Web Notoriety: Moral Contemplations

As the peculiarity of web feline big names keeps on thriving, moral contemplations have come to the very front. The line between sharing the delight of feline friendship and taking advantage of these creatures for online substance and business gain has become progressively obscured.

Inquiries regarding the prosperity of felines exposed to the tensions of online notoriety, the obligations of proprietors, and the expected adverse consequences on cat government assistance have ignited significant discussions inside internet based networks.

Guaranteeing that the government assistance of the feline overshadows its web-based persona has turned into a key thought. Finding some kind of harmony between sharing awesome minutes and regarding the normal necessities and ways of behaving of the feline is basic to keep up with the moral respectability of web feline VIP culture.

The Fate of Web Feline Superstars: Patterns and Changes

As we explore the current scene of web feline superstars, considering the direction of this phenomenon is significant. Will felines keep on overwhelming the computerized domain, or would we say we are near the precarious edge of a change in web VIP culture? The developing elements of online entertainment, changing crowd inclinations, and cultural qualities will without a doubt shape the eventual fate of web feline big names.

The development of new stages, progressions in innovation, and advancing social patterns will add to the change of web feline VIP culture. Whether it's the ascent of computer generated reality encounters including darling cat friends or the investigation of imaginative ways of drawing in crowds, what's in store vows to be dynamic and capricious.

3. How Cats Became Cultural Icons

In the huge embroidered artwork of human culture, felines have woven themselves into the actual texture of our shared awareness, arising not just as pets yet as famous images with significant social importance. From the sacrosanct felines of old developments to the loved cat divinities of folklore and the cutting edge web sensations, the excursion of how felines became social symbols is a charming investigation of the getting through connection among people and these perplexing animals.

Old Felines: Gatekeepers of Magic and Imagery

The catlike venture into social iconography starts in the old world, where felines held a holy and enchanted status. In old Egypt, felines were loved for their effortlessness and saw divine association. The goddess Bastet, frequently portrayed as a lioness or with the top of a homegrown feline, represented home, ripeness, and insurance. Felines were kept as pets as well as were viewed as gatekeepers against abhorrent spirits.

The Egyptians' adoration for felines reached out to their entombment rehearses, for certain felines getting intricate memorial services and burial chambers. This social importance mirrored the conviction that felines had an otherworldly pith, highlighting their job as the two mates and images of a more profound, magical association.

Felines in Folklore: Dreams and Otherworldly Creatures

As civic establishments advanced, so did the job of felines in folklore. In Norse folklore, the goddess Freyja, related with adoration, magnificence, and fruitfulness, had a chariot that was drawn by two enormous felines. This affiliation raised felines to the situation with divine sidekicks, featuring their association with the supernatural and the ethereal.

Essentially, in Japanese fables, the magical animal known as the "Bakeneko" or "Nekomata" addressed a heavenly feline with shape-moving capacities. These legendary creatures exhibited the duality frequently connected with felines in old stories — animals that could be both standard and unprecedented, trained and secretive.

Felines in Craftsmanship: Tasteful Motivations and Emblematic Portrayals

As craftsmanship turned into a strong mode for social articulation, felines tracked down their direction onto materials and figures. In the workmanship world, felines became emblematic portrayals of different characteristics — from effortlessness and polish to secret and freedom. Popular craftsmen like Edouard Manet, Théophile

Steinlen, and Leonardo da Vinci deified felines in their works, catching the embodiment of these animals and lifting them to social images.

In the Japanese ukiyo-e woodblock prints, felines became well known subjects, frequently depicted as fun loving partners or magical creatures. These imaginative portrayals commended the tasteful allure of felines as well as added to their social imagery as animals of magnificence and interest.

Felines in Writing: Abstract Symbols and Emblematic Moral stories

The composed word additionally hardened the social meaning of felines. In writing, felines rose above their jobs as simple creatures and became artistic symbols. The devilish Cheshire Feline from Lewis Carroll's "Alice's Experiences in Wonderland" and the shrewd and mysterious feline in J.K. Rowling's "Harry Potter" series are instances of how felines have been utilized as representative figures, typifying characteristics like secret, intelligence, and eccentricity.

Felines likewise assumed a huge part in T.S. Eliot's "Old Possum's Book of Useful Felines," which filled in as the motivation for the prestigious melodic "Felines" by Andrew Lloyd Webber. The characters in Eliot's sonnets, each with its extraordinary character, exhibited the different features of cat nature and added to the social impression of felines as multi-layered creatures.

Felines in Religion: Watchmen and Representative Partners

The impact of felines reaches out into strict imagery, where they are frequently depicted as gatekeepers or emblematic partners. In Islam, felines are viewed as spotless creatures, and the Prophet Muhammad is said to have had a profound warmth for them.

In Japanese Shintoism, felines are accepted to have otherworldly characteristics, and the "Maneki-neko" or enticing feline is a well known charm that is remembered to bring best of luck and fortune.

The presence of felines in strict imagery highlights their novel status as animals that span the everyday and the heavenly. Their depiction as defenders and images of favorable luck supports the social impression of felines as creatures with an extraordinary association with the profound domain.

The Feline's Renaissance: From Social Image to Web Sensation

While felines have kept up with their representative presence from the beginning of time, the cutting edge period has seen a renaissance in the manner they are seen and celebrated. The coming of the web shot felines into another domain of social importance, changing them from conventional images to worldwide sensations.

The peculiarity of well known web felines, like Cantankerous Feline, Lil Buddy, and Nyan Feline, denoted a change in perspective in how felines are embraced as social symbols. The far and wide sharing of feline recordings, images, and pictures made a worldwide local area of feline lovers, rising above geological and social limits.

Cantankerous Feline: The Essence of Web Cat Popularity

Cantankerous Feline, with her ceaselessly disappointed articulation, turned into a web sensation in 2012. The picture of her frowning face immediately became famous online, prompting an outpouring of images, product, and media appearances. Testy Feline, whose genuine name was Tardar Sauce, turned into an image of online culture, catching the humor and incongruity that saturates the computerized scene.

What made Surly Feline a social symbol was her look as well as the engaging and hilarious inscriptions that went with her pictures. The persona made around Testy Feline resounded with individuals around the world, changing her into an image of regular dissatisfactions and a wellspring of entertainment.

Lil Pal: An Image of Singularity and Acknowledgment

Lil Buddy, with her one of a kind appearance because of hereditary peculiarities, turned into one more darling figure in the realm of web felines. Her charming highlights, including a ceaselessly jutting tongue, made her in a flash unmistakable and charmed her to a large number of fans. Lil Pal's proprietor, Mike Bridavsky, utilized her web popularity to bring issues to light about extraordinary requirements pets and advance acknowledgment and understanding.

Lil Pal's excursion exhibited the force of web felines to cultivate positive social effect. Her presence in the computerized domain engaged as well as tested cultural standards and generalizations, adding to an additional comprehensive and caring social story.

Nyan Feline and the Ascent of Feline Images

Nyan Feline, an enlivened feline with a Pop-Tart body leaving a rainbow trail, turned into a notable image that typified the impulsive notion and silliness of web culture. The irresistible Nyan Feline melody, joined with the brilliant and dull movement, turned into a viral sensation. Nyan Feline embodies how web felines have risen above conventional imagery to turn out to be mainstream society peculiarities, catching the minds of millions and rousing an influx of innovative remixes and transformations.

The Brain research of Feline Allure: A Wellspring of Euphoria and Solace

The broad allure of felines, both in conventional imagery and as web superstars, can be credited to the mental and profound associations they manufacture with people. Felines have a one of a kind blend of qualities — from their fun loving tricks and effortless developments to their free yet tender nature — that reverberate with individuals on a profound and instinctive level.

Research recommends that watching feline recordings can emphatically affect temperament and decrease pressure and uneasiness. The web's interest with felines should be visible as an aggregate reaction to the helpful euphoria and solace these animals bring. Whether in old imagery or present day images, the social iconography of felines takes advantage of a widespread human yearning for association, entertainment, and profound prosperity.

Felines as Persevering through Social Symbols

The excursion of how felines became social symbols is a demonstration of the persevering and multi-layered nature of the catlike human relationship. From old imagery and folklore to the computerized time of web sensations, felines have reliably involved an extraordinary spot in the human mind.

As social images, felines epitomize a rich embroidery of implications — from secret and intelligence to fun loving nature and freedom. The web period has not lessened these representative characteristics but rather has, as a matter of fact, intensified and changed them into a worldwide peculiarity. Web felines have turned into a wellspring of diversion, motivation, and social change, enrapturing the hearts of millions and forming the social scene in exceptional ways.

Eventually, whether through the eyes of old civic establishments, the strokes of imaginative experts, or the pixels of web images, felines have become social symbols as well as getting through sidekicks on the common excursion of mankind. The mysterious appeal of felines, with their ageless appeal and erratic impulses, guarantees that their place as social symbols will proceed to advance and flourish in the hearts and minds of ages to come.

Chapter 1

Internet Cat Celebrities

The web has demonstrated to be a gold mine of diversion, and among its stars, an unconventional classification has arisen - Web Feline VIPs. These catlike sensations have pawed their direction into the hearts of millions, making a peculiarity that goes past the universe of charming pet recordings. This article dives into the charming universe of Web Feline VIPs, investigating their ascent to notoriety, the stages that launch them into the spotlight, and the significant effect they've had on our computerized culture.

II. Verifiable Point of view

The interest with felines on the web is definitely not a new turn of events. The beginning of online culture saw the rise of feline related content, from pictures to recordings. In any case, it was only after the multiplication of online entertainment stages that felines really became computerized superstars. The advancement of feline substance can be followed from straightforward pictures to complex recordings, establishing the groundwork for the famous feline superstars we know today.

III. Qualities of Web Feline Superstars

What separates these catlike stars? Their appeal lies in a mix of significant qualities and ways of behaving. Whether it's Cranky Feline's unendingly crotchety articulation or Maru's adoration for plunging into boxes, these felines have an extraordinary mystique that resounds with crowds. The close to home association watchers feel towards these web sensations adds a layer of appeal, transforming them into something other than viral recordings.

IV. Stages and Virtual Entertainment

The ascent of Web Feline Superstars is innately attached to the stages that feature their jokes. YouTube, Instagram, Twitter, and TikTok have become virtual stages where these felines perform for their crowd. The job of client created content couldn't possibly be more significant, as feline proprietors and lovers add to the steadily developing pool of feline related material.

V. Eminent Web Feline Superstars

Crotchety Feline

Crotchety Feline, with her interminably surly articulation because of cat dwarfism, turned into an out of the blue phenomenon. The unmistakable look sent off her into fame, bringing about a tremendous product domain and media appearances.

Nyan Feline

Nyan Feline, an enlivened feline with a Pop-Tart body, accomplished distinction through a circling GIF and infectious music. Its web image status and effect on mainstream society make it an eminent figure in the realm of online felines.

Lil Pal

Lil Pal, known for her one of a kind appearance because of hereditary transformations, acquired notoriety for her inspiring story and magnanimous endeavors. Her process motivated a dedicated fanbase and featured the positive effect feline famous people can have.

Maru

Maru, a Scottish Crease feline from Japan, enchanted the world with his adoration for boxes. His energetic shenanigans and charming character prompted a monstrous following, displaying the worldwide idea of web feline distinction.

Console Feline

An early web sensation, Console Feline acquired notoriety through recordings highlighting the feline "playing" an electronic console. The image became inseparable from startling or comical circumstances, cementing its place in web history.

Pusheen

Pusheen, a plump dark feline person, turned into a web dear through charming webcomics. The person's far and wide allure converted into stock, delineating the business capability of feline superstars.

Simon's Feline

Simon's Feline, a beguiling energized series made by Simon Tofield, follows the misfortunes of a feline and his proprietor. The interesting situations inspired an emotional response from feline proprietors around the world, making it a cherished establishment.

VI. The Feline Big name Industry

The fame of these catlike sensations reaches out past viral recordings. The feline big name industry has prospered, with amazing open doors for marketing and marking arriving at phenomenal levels. Feline big names have changed into powerhouses, teaming up with brands and utilizing their prevalence to draw in crowds in creative ways.

VII. The Brain science Behind Feline Recordings

For what reason truly do individuals adore watching feline recordings? The mental effect of feline substance on watchers is an entrancing perspective to investigate. Studies recommend that watching feline recordings can further develop state of mind and diminish feelings of anxiety. Felines, with their eccentric way of behaving and cute shenanigans, act as virtual treatment in an undeniably computerized world.

VIII. Influence on Feline Reception

The positive impact of feline superstars reaches out to the domain of creature government assistance. Many feline superstars are taken on creatures, and their accounts move incalculable people to consider embracing from covers. The harmonious connection between feline famous people and feline reception grandstands the potential for advanced stages to drive certifiable change.

IX. Difficulties and Contentions

Nonetheless, the universe of web feline famous people isn't without its difficulties. Concerns in regards to the likely abuse of these creatures and the moral ramifications of involving them for online substance have started discusses. Finding some kind of harmony among diversion and creature government assistance is urgent to keeping up with the respectability of the feline big name peculiarity.

X. Future Patterns and Improvements

As innovation propels, so does the scene of web feline acclaim. Arising feline superstars keep on catching the consideration of online crowds, and mechanical developments open additional opportunities for making and consuming feline substance. What's in store guarantees an astonishing advancement in the manner in which we cooperate with and commend our computerized cat colleagues.

1.1Grumpy Cat: The Face of Feline Sass

In the tremendous universe of web sensations, few have accomplished the famous status of Surly Feline. Known for her interminably disappointed articulation, Irritable Feline, whose genuine name was Tardar Sauce, rose above the domain of viral images to turn into a social peculiarity. This exposition digs into the charming excursion of Irritable Feline, investigating the starting points of her internet based notoriety, the effect she had on mainstream society, and the enduring inheritance she abandons.

1. Presentation

Surly Feline, with her unmistakably malcontented face, arose as a web sensation in 2012. Claimed by Tabatha Bundesen, the feline's extraordinary appearance earned consideration via online entertainment stages, in the end catapulting her to global fame. This paper plans to unwind the tale of Irritable Feline, analyzing the elements that added to her ascent, the persona that caught the hearts of millions, and the more extensive ramifications of her distinction.

2. **The Unassuming Starting points**

The narrative of Crotchety Feline's ascent to notoriety starts with a straightforward picture posted on Reddit in 2012. A photo exhibiting Tardar Sauce's unendingly irritable face immediately built up some momentum, drawing the consideration of clients who were dazzled by the feline's exceptional demeanor. Much to anyone's dismay that this modest post would check the start of an excursion that would transform Surly Feline into a worldwide sensation.

3. **The Ascent to Global Fame**

The fast climb of Surly Feline from a dark Reddit post to worldwide fame is a demonstration of the force of the web and the viral idea of online substance. Images highlighting Grouchy Feline's picture flowed quickly across different web-based entertainment stages, catching the minds of clients around the world. The feline's particular frown and the clever inscriptions added by fans changed her into a computerized big name, with a great many individuals sharing and drawing in with her substance.

4. **The Cantankerous Feline Persona**

What put Cantankerous Feline aside was her actual appearance as well as the persona that arose around her. Fans humanized her crotchety articulation, crediting a cheeky and snide demeanor to the catlike superstar. Images highlighting Irritable Feline were not just pictures of a feline; they were articulations of general discontent, entertainingly catching the disappointments and inconveniences of regular daily existence.

5. **Business Achievement**

Grouchy Feline's fame was not bound to the computerized domain. Perceiving the business capability of her novel image, the Bundesen family profited by Grouchy Feline's notoriety. The feline's resemblance was authorized for a bunch of items, including shirts, mugs, toys, and, surprisingly, a line of Cantankerous Feline enlivened refreshments. The product realm that arose around Irritable Feline showed the attractiveness of web feline superstars and their capacity to rise above the internet based world.

6. **Virtual Entertainment and Worldwide Impact**

Virtual entertainment assumed an essential part in enhancing Surly Feline's worldwide impact. The feline's true web-based entertainment accounts, oversaw by the Bundesen family, amassed great many supporters. Standard updates, shrewd subtitles, and commitment with fans developed a gave online local area. Cantankerous Feline turned into a social standard, with her pictures and images shared across landmasses, rising above language obstructions and social contrasts.

7. **Influence on Mainstream society**

Grouchy Feline's effect on mainstream society was significant. Her grouchy face turned into a quickly conspicuous image of web humor. References to Surly Feline's appearance pervaded regular discussions, tracking down their direction into images, gifs, and, surprisingly, customary media. The feline's picture was highlighted in plugs, network shows, and, surprisingly, a made-for-television film, hardening her status as a famous figure of modern times.

8. **Behind the Crab: Tardar Sauce's Genuine Story**

Underneath the cantankerous façade introduced to the world, Tardar Sauce was a darling family pet. The Bundesen family underscored that Cranky Feline's web-based persona didn't precisely mirror her actual attitude. Depicted as sweet, loving, and delicate, Tardar Sauce tested the presumptions made in light of her surly articulation. Her story featured the dissimilarity between online personas and the truth of these web superstars' lives.

9. **The Tradition of Cranky Feline**

Unfortunately, Crotchety Feline died in May 2019 at seven years old. In spite of her takeoff, the tradition of Surly Feline perseveres. Her effect on web culture, the feline VIP industry, and society's view of online cat friendship stays discernible. Cantankerous Feline prepared for other feline VIPs, demonstrating that the web could transform a customary feline into a worldwide symbol.

10. **The Feline Big name Industry**

Irritable Feline's prosperity contributed altogether to the advancement of the feline VIP industry. The exceptional commercialization of her image set a trend for other web popular cats. Brands perceived the showcasing capability of cooperating with feline powerhouses, prompting a flood in coordinated efforts and further obscuring the lines among conventional and computerized publicizing.

11. **Reactions and Contentions**

Surly Feline's prosperity was not without its portion of reactions. Concerns were raised about the expected abuse of the feline for business gain. Creature government assistance advocates scrutinized the morals of involving creatures for online substance, particularly when attached to benefit. The contentions encompassing Irritable Feline provoked conversations about the obligations of pet people who push their creatures into the spotlight.

1.2Lil Bub: The Cat with Perma-Kitten Charm

In the chronicles of web legend, the narrative of Lil Pal unfurls as an endearing excursion that started in June 2011 in provincial Indiana. Found as the half-pint of a wild litter, Lil Pal's novel hereditary cosmetics and spellbinding appeal set up for a catlike peculiarity that would catch the hearts of millions all over the planet.

The Early Battles

Lil Pal's story initiates with her modest starting points as the littlest and most fragile individual from her litter. Brought into the world with unmistakable hereditary peculiarities, including dwarfism and osteoporosis, she confronted early difficulties that might have hindered her way to joy. Notwithstanding, her encourage parental figure, Mike Bridavsky, perceived the unprecedented in the conventional and chose to give Lil Buddy the consideration and love she expected to flourish.

Perma-Little cat Enchantment Uncovered

What makes Lil Pal really unique is her perma-cat enchant, an immortal quality that radiates from her never-endingly little size and charming elements. The web quickly embraced her as an image of never-ending kittenhood, with her particular appearance - from captivating eyes to a tongue that generally looked out - transforming Lil Buddy into an internet based vibe that rose above the limits of the computerized world.

Emanating Energy and Love

Lil Pal's charm stretches out past her actual appearance. Notwithstanding wrestling with wellbeing challenges, she turned into a reference point of energy and love. Her online entertainment presence turned into a demonstration of the delight she found in day to day exercises, whether playing with toys or snuggling with everyone around her. Lil Buddy's irresistible joy reverberated with fans, making her in excess of a feline; she turned into a wellspring of motivation and trust.

Exploring Unique Requirements

Lil Pal's interesting hereditary arrangement required exceptional consideration. Challenges originating from osteoporosis and an immature jaw incited her parental figures to make a particular eating regimen and give careful regard for her prosperity. Regardless of these impediments, Lil Pal's versatility and the devoted consideration she got permitted her not exclusively to make due yet to thrive, displaying the groundbreaking force of affection and responsibility.

Rising to Superstar Status

Lil Buddy's prominence prospered past the computerized domain, raising her to big name status. Her charming face enhanced a plenty of product, including extravagant toys and schedules. Images including Lil

Buddy circled across the web, and she showed up at occasions and on TV programs. Lil Buddy's excursion from a web sensation to a social peculiarity made a permanent imprint on mainstream society, displaying the all inclusive allure of her perma-little cat fascinate.

Support and Raising money

Past giving pleasure to millions, Lil Pal's effect appeared in unmistakable ways. Her guardians laid out the Lil Buddy's Huge Asset, a beneficent association devoted to supporting creature havens and drives for creatures out of luck. Through different gathering pledges tries, Lil Pal's impact reached out past the virtual world, making a positive imprint on the existences of various creatures and bringing issues to light about the consideration of exceptional requirements pets.

Lil Buddy's Enduring Inheritance

Sadly, Lil Pal crossed the rainbow span in December 2019, abandoning a heritage that keeps on resounding. While her actual presence might have left, Lil Pal's memory lives on through recognitions, fan workmanship, and the incalculable minutes she imparted to the world. Her perma-little cat enchant and immovable soul persevere, guaranteeing that the effect she made on the web-based local area stays a getting through demonstration of the force of bliss and love.

Molding Web Culture

Lil Buddy's impact reaches out past her charming appearance. She assumed a urgent part in forming web culture, adding to the ascent of "feline powerhouses." This pattern has prompted the far reaching acknowledgment of cat big names on stages like Instagram and TikTok. Lil Pal's prosperity prepared for a social interest with enchanting and particular felines, making a getting through imprint on the steadily developing scene of online substance.

The Proceeding with Veneration for Lil Pal

Indeed, even in her actual nonappearance, Lil Pal's memory is kept alive by the continued flood of affection from fans. Web-based entertainment stages act as materials for accolades and legacy posts, highlighting the profound association individuals framed with her exceptional and adorable character. Lil Pal's getting through prevalence repeats the significant effect she had on the web-based local area, making an enduring connection between the perma-little cat symbol and her loving crowd.

Illustrations from Lil Pal

Lil Buddy's story gives important illustrations about acknowledgment, flexibility, and the groundbreaking force of energy. Her excursion from a defenseless, unique necessities little cat to a worldwide sensation fills in as a strong sign of the effect that consideration and cherish can have on people, regardless of actual contrasts. Lil Pal's heritage urges us to commend uniqueness and find euphoria in the straightforward minutes, leaving a never-ending paw print on the world.

Lil Buddy - The Timeless Perma-Little cat Symbol

All in all, Lil Pal arises as a timeless perma-cat symbol, her story winding around an embroidery of motivation, delight, and support. From her unassuming starting points to her ascent as a worldwide sensation, Lil Buddy's process embodies the groundbreaking force of affection and the getting through effect of a little feline with perma-cat enchant. As the web keeps on developing, Lil Pal's heritage stays carved in the aggregate memory of the people who were sufficiently lucky to observe the sorcery of this exceptional cat.

1.3 Nyan Cat and the Birth of Internet Memes

In the huge scene of the web, where data, thoughts, and imagination impact, the introduction of images has turned into a captivating part of online culture. Images, in their different structures, have turned into their very own language, rising above conventional specialized techniques. One such famous image that caught the web's consideration and turned into a social peculiarity is the Nyan Feline.

1. The Beginning of Nyan Feline: A Viral Sensation

It was 2011 when a curious, rainbow-shaded feline with a Pop-Tart body and a path of pixelated exhaust graced the screens of web clients around the world. This energized catlike, known as Nyan Feline, rose up out of the profundities of the web, leaving a path of infectious tunes and an inheritance that would rise above its unique setting.

1. **Beginnings of Nyan Feline**

   Nyan Feline's process started when a client named Chris Torres transferred a GIF movement to the site Haha Comics on April 2, 2011. The person was a combination of a Japanese pop-tart feline, frequently alluded to as "nyanko" or "nyan," and the idea of a Pop-Tart, an American breakfast baked good. Torres' creation was joined by a circled soundtrack including a snappy Japanese tune known as "Nyanyanyanyanyanyanya!" by Daniwell-P.

2. **Viral Spread and Remix Culture**

Nyan Feline's fame soar as clients across different internet based stages, especially YouTube, embraced the eccentric cat. The image's circled liveliness and irresistible soundtrack added to its viral nature, making it a #1 among web clients. Also, the image's versatility prompted a blast of remixes, with clients inventively adjusting the first Nyan Feline to fit various subjects, music classes, and mainstream society references.

II. Life structures of an Image: Grasping Nyan Feline's Allure

1. **The Feel of Nyan Feline**

   Nyan Feline's visual allure assumed a critical part in its far reaching reception. The mix of splendid, energetic tones, an oversimplified at this point charming feline plan, and the entrancing rainbow trail made an eye-getting scene. The pixel craftsmanship stylish added a nostalgic touch, harkening back to early computer games and web illustrations, reverberating with a different crowd.

2. **The Force of Reiteration and Infectious Tunes**

   Images frequently flourish with reiteration and effortlessness, and Nyan Feline was no exemption. The circled activity, combined with the monotonous "nyan" soundtrack, instilled itself into the personalities of the people who experienced it. The habit-forming nature of the tune and the unending circle added to the image's backbone, guaranteeing it stayed in the shared awareness of the web.

3. All inclusiveness and Openness

One of Nyan Feline's assets as an image was its all inclusive allure. The shortfall of language obstructions permitted it to rise above social and etymological limits. Anybody, no matter what their experience, could see the value in the fanciful notion of a flying feline leaving a rainbow trail. This all inclusiveness added to the image's quick dispersal and reception across assorted web-based networks.

III. Nyan Feline in Mainstream society

1. Standard Acknowledgment

As Nyan Feline kept on overwhelming internet based spaces, it advanced into traditional press. The image turned into an image of web culture, referred to in TV programs, plugs, and, surprisingly, integrated into computer games. Nyan Feline's impact arrived at unforeseen corners of mainstream society, hardening its place as a famous figure in the computerized scene.

2. Promoting and Commercialization

The inescapable fame of Nyan Feline prompted different promoting open doors. The picture of the rainbow-following feline found its direction onto Shirts, extras, and other product, permitting fans to communicate their adoration for the image in unmistakable ways. This commercialization denoted a change in the web image scene, where images started to rise above their computerized beginnings and enter the actual world.

IV. The Tradition of Nyan Feline: Past the Image

1. Influence on Web Culture

Nyan Feline's inheritance goes past its status as a viral image. It assumed a critical part in forming the developing scene of web culture. The image's prosperity featured the force of client produced content and the capacity of web networks to embrace and proliferate shared encounters by and large.

2. **Nyan Feline as an Image of Wistfulness**

The pixelated stylish of Nyan Feline took advantage of a feeling of sentimentality for early web clients who grew up with straightforward illustrations and simple livelinesss. In a quickly impacting computerized world, Nyan Feline gave a nostalgic anchor, helping clients to remember an easier time on the web.

3. **Development and Perseverance**

While web images frequently have a short life expectancy, Nyan Feline has resisted the chances and persevered in the aggregate memory of online networks. Its capacity to adjust to evolving patterns, stay applicable through remixes, and find new crowds shows the image's flexibility and progressing influence.

V. Nyan Feline's Persevering through Excursion

In the chronicles of web history, Nyan Feline stands apart as a demonstration of the flighty and dynamic nature of online culture. From its unassuming starting points as a GIF on a satire site to turning into an internationally perceived image, Nyan Feline's process epitomizes the quintessence of web images.

Its vivid and eccentric presence keeps on inspiring grins, trigger wistfulness, and act as a wake up call of the web's capacity to make and engender social peculiarities.

As we consider the introduction of Nyan Feline and the more extensive peculiarity of web images, it becomes clear that these computerized manifestations are not simply momentary minutes but rather social relics that leave an enduring engraving on the consistently developing scene of the internet based world. Nyan Feline, with its rainbow trail and infectious tune, stays a treasured symbol, taking off through the web's tremendous region and abandoning a heritage that rises above the pixels and codes from which it was conceived.

Chapter 2

Cats in Social Media

In the consistently growing domain of web-based entertainment, where quality written substance makes all the difference and commitment rules, it's irrefutable that felines have ripped at their way to the front of online consideration. From the beginning of the web to the present, cat mates have developed from simple family pets to virtual entertainment hotshots, spellbinding crowds, motivating images, and making a computerized subculture based on the compelling appeal of felines. This investigation dives into the multi-layered job of felines in web-based entertainment, looking at their ascent to conspicuousness, the brain science behind their fame, the effect on web culture, and the more extensive ramifications of this catlike peculiarity.

1. **The Development of Felines on the Web**
1. **From Charming Feline Photographs to Viral Recordings**
   The web's relationship with felines didn't come about more or less by accident. It started with the expansion of charming feline photographs shared on early friendly stages and discussions. These charming pictures took advantage of the widespread allure

of delightful creatures, encouraging a feeling of bliss and idealism for watchers. As web transfer speed expanded, the time of viral feline recordings arose, catching the consideration of a world-wide crowd.

2. **The Development of Feline Images**

The web's image culture assumed a urgent part in catapulting felines into the online entertainment spotlight. Images like "I Can Has Cheezburger?" and "Surly Feline" became notable, with clients embracing the diverting subtitles and engaging articulations of cat heroes. These images engaged as well as made a common language among web clients, adding to the feeling of local area inside internet based spaces.

3. **Ascent of Feline Forces to be reckoned with**

As web-based entertainment stages advanced, felines progressed from periodic viral stars to reliable substance makers with committed followings. Stages like Instagram and YouTube became favorable places for feline powerhouses — cat accounts show to pet people that amassed huge crowds. These powerhouses utilized their felines' characters, feel, and tricks to construct connected with networks, preparing for another time of advanced cat distinction.

II. The Brain science Behind Feline Ubiquity

1. **Profound Association and Solace**

The web's fixation on felines isn't simply a shallow pattern; it's well established in human brain science. Research proposes that pictures and recordings of felines trigger good feelings, including sensations of warmth, happiness, and unwinding. In a speedy and frequently unpleasant computerized scene, felines give an encouraging and cheerful getaway, cultivating a feeling of close to home association among clients and their cat advanced sidekicks.

2. **Appeal and Humor**

Felines' ways of behaving, articulations, and characteristics make them exceptionally interesting to a different crowd. Whether it's the reserved quality of a feline disregarding its proprietor or the energetic jokes of a little cat, these engaging minutes make a common encounter among watchers. Furthermore, the humor intrinsic in many feline related images and recordings fills in as a general language, rising above social and semantic hindrances.

3. Helpful Worth of Feline Substance

Past amusement, the helpful worth of feline substance via online entertainment couldn't possibly be more significant. Studies have demonstrated the way that watching feline recordings can decrease pressure and increment sensations of bliss. The quieting impact of noticing a feline's delicate murmuring or energetic way of behaving adds to the pattern of integrating felines into computerized spaces intended for unwinding and mental prosperity.

III. Felines as Social Impetuses

1. Forming Web Culture

Felines play had a crucial impact in forming the language and culture of the web. The reception of feline related emoticons, the utilization of feline images in web-based discussions, and the formation of devoted feline themed subcultures all validate the getting through impact of cat colleagues on the computerized scene. Felines have become social impetuses, igniting patterns and motivating inventiveness across different internet based networks.

2. Marketing and Commercialization

The notoriety of felines via online entertainment has risen above the advanced domain, prompting broad promoting open doors. Feline themed items, from dress and assistants to home stylistic layout and pet supplies, have overwhelmed the market. Feline powerhouses frequently team up with brands, further obscuring the lines between online substance creation and business adventures.

The commercialization of felines in virtual entertainment brings up issues about the commodification of pets and the morals encompassing their web-based presence.

IV. Difficulties and Debates

1. **Morals of Feline Forces to be reckoned with**

   The ascent of feline forces to be reckoned with has incited conversations about the moral contemplations of transforming pets into online famous people. Worries about the prosperity of the creatures, the potential for double-dealing, and the effect of distinction on their lives have energized banters inside internet based networks. Finding some kind of harmony between sharing delightful substance and guaranteeing the government assistance of cat forces to be reckoned with has turned into a major problem in the time of computerized pet fame.

2. **Duping and Tricks**

The prominence of feline substance has led to an unconventional peculiarity known as "duping," where people use pictures or recordings of felines to make misleading web-based personas. This training brings up issues about character, genuineness, and the obscured lines among the real world and online fiction. The clueless crowd might end up brought into intricate tricks, featuring the hazier side of the web's interest with cat associates.

V. Future Patterns and Contemplations

1. **Proceeded with Development of Feline Substance**

   As web-based entertainment stages develop, so too will the idea of feline substance. Virtual and increased reality advances might offer new ways for clients to collaborate with computerized felines, further obscuring the limits between the on the web and disconnected universes. The reconciliation of man-made consciousness may likewise add to the production of more customized and intuitive feline related encounters.

2. Moral Rules and Dependable Pet Proprietorship

With the rising noticeable quality of feline powerhouses, the requirement for moral rules and mindful pet proprietorship in the advanced age becomes urgent. Online entertainment stages, pet people, and crowds should work cooperatively to lay out guidelines that focus on the government assistance and prosperity of the creatures in question. This remembers contemplations for the effect of distinction for pets, the utilization of creatures in promoting, and the likely double-dealing of their pictures.

VI.Cats as Computerized Buddies

In the huge embroidery of online entertainment, felines have arisen as something other than charming mates — they have become advanced symbols, social images, and wellsprings of bliss for millions. From the beginning of the web to the present, the excursion of felines in virtual entertainment mirrors the developing elements of online culture, the force of shared encounters, and the mind boggling transaction between innovation, brain science, and human association.

As we explore the steadily growing scene of online entertainment, the presence of felines stays a consistent, offering a string of coherence in the always changing computerized story. Whether they are carrying a grin to our countenances, filling in as wellsprings of solace, or igniting conversations about morals and online culture, felines have solidly secured themselves as vital individuals from the web-based entertainment environment, leaving their permanent paw prints on the hearts and screens of clients all over the planet.

2.1Instagram Cats: Purr-sonalities with a Global Following

In the unique domain of virtual entertainment, one stage stands apart as a sanctuary for cat devotees and admirers of charming substance the same — Instagram. The photograph driven stage has led to a peculiarity where felines have become pets as well as computerized murmur sonalities with dedicated worldwide followings. This investigation digs into the universe of Instagram felines, analyzing the variables behind their notoriety, the ascent of feline forces to be reckoned with, the effect on web culture, moral contemplations, and what's in store patterns forming this great corner of the web.

1. **The Instagram Feline Blast: From Photographs to Murmur sonal Brands**
1. **The Charm of Instagram for Feline Proprietors**
   Instagram's visual nature, usability, and accentuation on narrating through pictures make it an optimal stage for feline proprietors to impart their catlike allies to the world. Early adopters of Instagram immediately found that the stage gave a phase to their felines to sparkle, exhibiting their peculiar ways of behaving, interesting characters, and, obviously, irrefutable charm.
2. **The Ascent of Feline Forces to be reckoned with**
   As feline proprietors started populating Instagram with great feline substance, another type of powerhouses arose — cat powerhouses. These felines, frequently oversaw by their human proprietors, began collecting supporters at an amazing rate. The mix of drawing in visuals, engaging subtitles, and vital utilization of hashtags transformed conventional felines into computerized superstars, with some accumulating supporter counts that rival those of human powerhouses.
3. **Variety in Murmur sonalities**

What makes Instagram felines so enthralling is the different scope of murmur sonalities they show. From the devilish shenanigans of courageous felines investigating nature to the majestic balance of refined indoor felines, every cat force to be reckoned with carries an extraordinary flavor to the stage. This variety in murmur sonalities adds to the wide allure of Instagram felines, permitting clients to find a catlike buddy that reverberates with their inclinations and sensibilities.

II. Factors Behind Instagram Feline Prevalence

1. **Stylish Allure: Visuals That Say a lot**
   The visual-driven nature of Instagram puts an exceptional on feel, and felines, with their intrinsically attractive characteristics, are an ideal fit for the stage. From enchanting little cats to lofty grown-up felines, the different exhibit of cat excellence adds to the wide allure of feline substance on Instagram.

2. **Appeal: Regular Minutes That Reverberate**
   One of the key variables driving the notoriety of Instagram felines is their appeal. Feline proprietors and devotees associate with the ordinary minutes caught in photographs and recordings — the energetic communications, the comfortable rests, the inquisitive investigations — all of which reflect the encounters of the people who share their lives with felines. This appeal cultivates a feeling of local area among devotees, making a common space for feline darlings to interface and lock in.

3. **Humor and Idiosyncrasy: Felines' Extraordinary Charms**
   Felines, with their unusual ways of behaving and peculiarities, bring a component of humor and idiosyncrasy to Instagram. Whether it's a feline endeavoring a gravity-resisting jump or getting into a case that appears to be tiny, these snapshots of cat imprudence resound with crowds looking for carefree and engaging substance.

4. **Profound Association: The Force of Feline Treatment**

Past the visual and entertaining allure, Instagram felines inspire a real close to home association with their crowd. Studies recommend that communicating with feline substance can set off sure feelings and decrease pressure. The quieting impact of watching a feline's delicate developments or partaking in a sincere second between a feline and its proprietor adds to the restorative worth that Instagram felines bring to clients' lives.

III. Feline Powerhouses and the Computerized Economy

1. Adaptation Amazing open doors

The prevalence of Instagram felines has led to a computerized economy where feline powerhouses can gain by their distinction. Supported posts, brand coordinated efforts, and associations with pet-related organizations offer income streams for feline proprietors. Furthermore, stock highlighting the resemblance of popular Instagram felines, from attire to extras, permits fans to communicate their affection for their number one cat powerhouses.

2. Difficulties of Commercialization

While the adaptation of Instagram felines gives open doors to their proprietors, it likewise brings up moral issues and difficulties. Adjusting the prosperity of the feline with the requests of brand organizations and the tensions of keeping a predictable internet based presence turns into a fragile undertaking. The line between certified content creation and business advancement should be painstakingly explored to guarantee the legitimacy of the feline powerhouse's murmur sonality.

IV. The Effect of Instagram Felines on Web Culture

1. Social Peculiarity and Shared Language

Instagram felines have risen above the domain of individual records to turn into a social peculiarity with its very own language. Hashtags like #CatsofInstagram and #InstaCat have become virtual social occasion places for feline devotees, cultivating a feeling of local area and shared appreciation for cat friendship. The language of feline images, emoticons, and web shoptalk connected with felines further shows their inescapable effect on web culture.

2. Molding Patterns Past Instagram

The impact of Instagram felines stretches out past the actual stage, molding patterns in mainstream society. From traditional press references to the mix of feline themed items on the lookout, the effect of these catlike powerhouses swells through different features of society. The capacity of Instagram felines to drive patterns features the advantageous connection between online culture and more extensive social articulations.

V. Moral Contemplations and Capable Pet Possession

1. **The Prosperity of Instagram Felines**
   The flood in feline powerhouses has ignited discussions about the moral contemplations encompassing their web-based presence. Inquiries concerning the prosperity of the felines, the effect of acclaim on their lives, and the obligations of their human proprietors have become central places of conversation inside internet based networks.
   Advocates for moral pet proprietorship underscore the significance of focusing on the government assistance of the felines over internet based notoriety.

2. **Adjusting Popularity and Prosperity**

Feline proprietors and powerhouses face the test of adjusting the requests of online popularity with the prosperity of their catlike mates. From dealing with the pressure of photoshoots to guaranteeing a protected and agreeable climate for the felines, mindful pet possession becomes central. Laying out moral rules for feline powerhouses and advancing straightforwardness in their practices are fundamental stages toward making a feasible and humane computerized biological system for Instagram felines.

VI. Future Patterns and the Development of Instagram Felines

1. **Progressions in Innovation: From Photographs to AR Encounters**

As innovation keeps on propelling, the manner in which clients communicate with Instagram felines is probably going to develop. Expanded reality (AR) encounters might permit adherents to basically "meet" their number one cat powerhouses in vivid ways. From intuitive channels to virtual play meetings, these innovative progressions could reclassify the idea of the advanced connection among felines and their worldwide crowd.

2. Local area Building and Commitment

The eventual fate of Instagram felines might see an expanded spotlight on local area building and commitment. Stages might foster highlights that work with associations among feline aficionados, making virtual spaces for conversations, occasions, and coordinated efforts. The feeling of local area encompassing Instagram felines could develop, cultivating associations that reach out past the computerized domain.

VII. Instagram Felines as Advanced Symbols

In the huge scene of web-based entertainment, Instagram felines have arisen as something beyond cute sidekicks — they are advanced symbols, social powerhouses, and wellsprings of delight for millions all over the planet. From their modest starting points as loved pets to their ongoing status as worldwide murmur sonalities, these catlike powerhouses have reclassified the manner in which we collaborate with and value the charming universe of felines.

As we explore the consistently developing domain of Instagram and the computerized scene in general, Instagram felines stand as a demonstration of the force of shared encounters, the delight of virtual associations, and the getting through allure of cat friendship.

From paw prints on hearts to a worldwide impression via web-based entertainment, Instagram felines keep on charming crowds, each cute post in turn, making a permanent imprint on the computerized embroidery of our interconnected world.

2.2 Cat Influencers: The Power of Fluffy Endorsements

In the far reaching universe of web-based entertainment, a one of a kind and compellingly beguiling peculiarity has arisen — the ascent of feline forces to be reckoned with. These cat computerized stars, with their cute tricks and magnetic murmur sonalities, have risen above the situation with family pets to turn out to be strong powerhouses, molding patterns, catching hearts, and making a rewarding industry. This investigation dives profound into the universe of feline forces to be reckoned with, analyzing the variables behind their ascent, the elements of their impact, the matter of cat popularity, moral contemplations, and the getting through effect of these soft supports on the advanced scene.

1. **The Murmur sistence of Feline Powerhouses: A Catlike Development**
1. **From House Felines to Virtual Entertainment Eminence**
   The excursion of feline powerhouses starts in family rooms and lawns, where standard house felines caught the hearts of their proprietors. With the approach of web-based entertainment, especially stages like Instagram, these cherished cat sidekicks changed from private relatives to public personas. The charm of sharing their idiosyncratic ways of behaving, enthralling articulations, and charming murmur sonalities made ready for another period of cat fame.
2. **Ascent of Feline Forces to be reckoned with: A Worldwide Peculiarity**
   The ascent of feline forces to be reckoned with is a worldwide peculiarity that knows no social or geographic limits. Felines from different foundations and breeds have collected global followings, making a virtual local area of feline darlings who rise above etymological, social, and segment contrasts. The worldwide allure of these catlike powerhouses adds to the production of a computerized space where the common love for felines turns into a binding together power.
3. **The Advanced Economy of Cat Distinction**

As the notoriety of feline forces to be reckoned with took off, a computerized economy encompassing cat distinction started to come to fruition. From brand joint efforts and supported content to stock deals and appearance expenses, feline powerhouses became central members in the steadily growing universe of force to be reckoned with showcasing. The matter of cat popularity has set out open doors for feline proprietors as well as laid out an extraordinary specialty inside the more extensive powerhouse scene.

II. The Life systems of Feline Impact: Elements Behind Their Notoriety

1. **Stylish Charm: Visual Allure and Attractive Ability**
   At the core of feline impact lies their obvious visual allure. Felines, with their attractive characteristics, beauty the screens of web-based entertainment clients with a tasteful appeal that is both beguiling and dazzling. The expressive eyes, lively postures, and fleecy layers of feline powerhouses add to a visual language that resounds with crowds looking for great and endearing substance.

2. **Appeal and Particularity: Making Computerized Associations**
   One of the key factors that fuel the ubiquity of feline powerhouses is their appeal. Felines, with their eccentric ways of behaving, lively tricks, and frequently reserved disposition, make a feeling of commonality for feline proprietors and lovers. The appeal of feline forces to be reckoned with cultivates an association between the computerized stars and their crowd, causing supporters to feel like they are partaking in the regular delights and difficulties of feline proprietorship.

3. **Profound Association: The Force of Feline Treatment**
   Past the visual and interesting allure, feline powerhouses inspire a certifiable close to home association with their devotees. The restorative benefit of watching felines participate in quieting exercises, from preparing meetings to delicate murmuring, gives a feeling of solace and delight. Feline powerhouses, with their capacity

to relieve and elevate spirits, become computerized sidekicks that offer a relief from the difficulties of day to day existence.

4. **Humor and Diversion: Cat Indiscretion In plain view**

Felines, with their capricious ways of behaving and perky nature, infuse a sound portion of humor and diversion into the computerized scene. Feline powerhouses frequently feature their catlike imprudence through entertaining recordings, unforeseen responses, and entertaining experiences with ordinary items. The cheerful and diverting substance made by feline powerhouses adds an upbeat component to the internet based insight, making a space for chuckling and grins.

III. The Matter of Cat Notoriety: Adapting Feline Impact

1. **Supported Content and Brand Joint efforts**
   One of the essential ways feline powerhouses adapt their distinction is through supported content and brand joint efforts. Organizations trying to take advantage of the tremendous and drew in crowd of feline powerhouses approach proprietors with offers to highlight their items or administrations.
   From feline food and accomplices to pet-accommodating travel and way of life brands, feline powerhouses become representatives for various items, making a commonly helpful connection among brands and cat stars.

2. **Promoting Valuable open doors: From Screens to Racks**
   The prevalence of feline forces to be reckoned with has converted into broad marketing open doors. Proprietors of popular felines frequently profit by their pet's picture by sending off stock lines highlighting all that from attire and accomplices to home stylistic theme and pet items. The marketing of feline powerhouses stretches out the advanced insight to the actual world, permitting fans to communicate their affection for their #1 cat stars in unmistakable ways.

3. **Appearance Charges and Occasions**

As feline powerhouses gain unmistakable quality, they become sought-after visitors for different occasions, both on the web and disconnected. From virtual meet-and-welcomes to face to face appearances at pet exhibitions and shows, feline powerhouses order appearance expenses for their time and star power. These occasions not just give chances to fans to associate with their #1 cat superstars yet additionally add to the general adaptation procedure of feline powerhouses.

4. **Crowdfunding and Fan Backing**

Some feline forces to be reckoned with go to crowdfunding stages and fan backing to enhance their pay. Stages like Patreon permit devotees to contribute monetarily to help the continuous production of feline substance. Consequently, allies frequently get select advantages like in the background access, customized whoops, and extraordinary substance made explicitly for the fan local area.

IV. Difficulties and Contentions in the Feline Force to be reckoned with Industry

1. **Moral Contemplations of Cat Popularity**

The quick development of the feline force to be reckoned with industry has delivered moral contemplations in regards to the government assistance and prosperity of the felines in question. Worries about the effect of popularity on the existences of these creatures, the pressure related with photoshoots and public appearances, and the by and large moral treatment of feline powerhouses have ignited conversations inside internet based networks and among creature government assistance advocates.

2. **Adjusting Realness and Commercialization**

Feline forces to be reckoned with and their proprietors face the test of finding some kind of harmony among credibility and commercialization. As the matter of cat distinction develops, there is a gamble of giving and taking the certifiable and unconstrained nature of feline substance for special organizations. Keeping up with the realness that charmed these felines to their crowd in any case turns into a fragile tightrope stroll in the serious scene of powerhouse showcasing.

3. **Wellbeing and Prosperity of Feline Forces to be reckoned with**

The wellbeing and prosperity of feline powerhouses are vital contemplations for dependable pet possession. The requests of the force to be reckoned with way of life, including incessant photoshoots, travel, and openness to new conditions, may influence the physical and psychological well-being of the felines. Proprietors and powerhouses should focus on the government assistance of their catlike mates, guaranteeing they have a protected and agreeable climate and are not exposed to excessive pressure for content creation.

V. Feline Powerhouses and Web Culture

1. **Molding Patterns Past the Catlike Specialty**
The impact of feline forces to be reckoned with stretches out past the limits of the catlike specialty, molding patterns in the more extensive scene of web culture. From traditional press references to the joining of feline themed items in different ventures, the effect of these cushioned endorsers comes to all over. The capacity of feline powerhouses to drive patterns features their job as social forces to be reckoned with the ability to shape shopper conduct and inclinations.

2. **Feline Images, Emoticons, and Advanced Language**

Feline powerhouses add to the production of a computerized language based on cat articulations. Feline images highlighting renowned forces to be reckoned with, custom feline emoticons, and web shoptalk connected with felines become basic pieces of online correspondence.

The language of feline impact turns into a social peculiarity, overcoming any issues between the computerized and genuine universes.

VI. The Eventual fate of Feline Powerhouses: Patterns and Contemplations

1. **Mechanical Headways: AR and Virtual Encounters**

   As innovation keeps on propelling, the eventual fate of feline powerhouses might see the incorporation of increased reality (AR) and virtual encounters. Devotees could associate with computerized variants of their number one feline powerhouses, making vivid and intuitive experiences.

   Virtual play meetings, expanded reality channels, and other innovative progressions could rethink the idea of the advanced connection among felines and their worldwide crowd.

2. **Local area Building and Commitment Elements**

   The eventual fate of feline powerhouses might include a more noteworthy accentuation on local area building and commitment highlights. Web-based entertainment stages might foster devices and functionalities that work with communications among feline aficionados, making virtual spaces for conversations, occasions, and joint efforts. The feeling of local area encompassing feline powerhouses could develop, encouraging associations that reach out past the computerized domain.

3. **Proceeded with Advancement of Feline Substance**

As the scene of online entertainment advances, feline powerhouses will probably adjust and enhance their substance to stay significant. From inventive narrating arrangements to coordinated efforts with other powerhouses, the adaptability of feline substance will add to the continuous commitment of their crowd. The proceeded with development of feline substance might include the investigation of new stages and arising advances, staying up with the steadily changing elements of computerized media.

2.3 Viral Cat Videos: From Keyboard Cat to Maru

In the tremendous computerized region of the web, scarcely any peculiarities have caught the aggregate hearts and consideration of clients very like viral feline recordings. From the beginning of web culture to the present, these cat driven cuts have turned into a social peculiarity, molding on the web patterns, rousing images, and exhibiting the compelling appeal of our shaggy friends. This investigation takes you on a magnificent excursion through the universe of viral feline recordings, investigating the trailblazers, the notable minutes, the development of the class, and the getting through effect of these unshaven stars.

1. **The Beginning of Viral Feline Recordings: Trailblazers and Antecedents**
1. **The Web's Liking for Felines**
   Felines have been a staple of web culture since its initial days. The web's relationship with cats can be followed back to the reception of felines as informal mascots for online discussions and networks. The charming and frequently erratic ways of behaving of felines made them a characteristic fit for the medium, prompting the making of early feline related content.
2. **Pre-YouTube Period: Feline GIFs and Streak Activitys**

Before the ascent of YouTube, feline related content essentially coursed as GIFs and Streak movements. These short, circling pictures and enlivened cuts displayed felines in different entertaining and lovable situations. The straightforwardness of these early configurations established the groundwork for the later blast of feline recordings on YouTube.

II. The YouTube Transformation: Feline Recordings Go Standard

1. **The Rise of YouTube as a Stage**
   The send off of YouTube in 2005 gave a devoted stage to sharing

and finding video content. As the stage acquired ubiquity, clients started transferring a variety of content, including a critical number of feline recordings. YouTube's easy to understand interface and simple sharing capacities assumed a pivotal part in the democratization of online video, permitting anybody with a camera to add to the developing scene of viral substance.

2. **Console Feline: A Spearheading Second**

One of the earliest popular feline recordings to acquire far and wide consideration was "Console Feline." Transferred in 2007 by Charlie Schmidt, the video highlighted a feline named Fatso playing an electronic console. The capricious mix of a feline playing an instrument evoked an emotional response from watchers and turned into an early illustration of the web's interest with felines in surprising and entertaining circumstances.

3. **Nyan Feline: The Introduction of an Image**

In 2011, the web saw the introduction of one more notorious viral feline video with the production of "Nyan Feline." This energized feline with a Pop-Tart body and a rainbow trail turned into a web sensation. The circled liveliness, set to an infectious Japanese tune, spellbound crowds and brought forth an influx of remixes and spoofs. Nyan Feline turned into an image of web culture and the force of images in molding on the web patterns.

III. Feline Famous people: Ascent of the Catlike Stars

1. **Cranky Feline: A Worldwide Sensation**

In 2012, the world was acquainted with the never-endingly disappointed face of Tardar Sauce, otherwise called Testy Feline. This extraordinary looking catlike immediately turned into a worldwide sensation, with her particular frown motivating images, product, and, surprisingly, a book bargain. Surly Feline's ascent to notoriety featured the web's propensity for felines with unmistakable highlights and characters.

2. **Maru: Japan's Most Popular Feline**
   Hailing from Japan, Maru became perhaps of the most cherished and conspicuous feline on the web. Known for his adoration for boxes and charming interest, Maru caught the hearts of watchers all over the planet. The straightforwardness and appeal of Maru's recordings exhibited the all inclusive allure of feline substance and added to the worldwide interest with Japanese feline culture.

3. **Lil Buddy, Colonel Whimper, and Other Cat Superstars**

Cantankerous Feline and Maru were in good company in their web-based fame. Felines like Lil Pal, known for her one of a kind appearance and generous endeavors, and Colonel Whimper, celebrated for his sumptuous fur and majestic disposition, became web VIPs by their own doing. The assorted characters and qualities of these catlike stars exhibited the expansiveness of allure inside the viral feline video class.

IV. Viral Feline Video Classifications: From Satire to Experience

1. **Comedic Feline Recordings: The Force of Humor**
   Numerous viral feline recordings influence the innate humor in cat ways of behaving. From felines responding to surprising boosts to perky communications with family things, comedic feline recordings tap into the widespread allure of chuckling. Important minutes, for example, felines seeming frightened by cucumbers or taking part in eccentric exercises, have become notable inside the class.

2. **Audacious Felines: Investigating Nature**
   Some feline recordings grandstand cats wandering into nature, showing their normal interest and readiness. Whether it's a feline investigating a nursery, climbing trees, or leaving on outside experiences, these recordings give a brief look into the brave side of our catlike companions. The juxtaposition of homegrown felines in outside settings adds a component of shock and miracle.

3. **Adorable and Endearing Minutes: Aww-moving Substance**

Charm and inspiring minutes have forever been a main thrust behind viral feline recordings. From cats finding the world to endearing collaborations among felines and their human colleagues, these recordings inspire warm sentiments and make a feeling of association. Such happy frequently goes past amusement, pulling at the heartstrings of watchers.

V. The Advancement of Feline Video Stages: Past YouTube

1. **Instagram and the Ascent of Feline Forces to be reckoned with**
   As web-based entertainment stages advanced, so did the scene of feline recordings. Instagram arose as a noticeable stage for short-structure visual substance, and feline powerhouses started to overwhelm the space. The stage's accentuation on visuals and narrating permitted feline proprietors to make drawing in accounts around their catlike friends, prompting the ascent of feline famous people with monstrous followings.

2. **TikTok: Short-Structure Feline Substance Becomes the overwhelming focus**
   TikTok, with its short-structure video design, turned into the most recent wilderness for viral feline substance. The stage's calculations and patterns led to another age of feline powerhouses, with clients making speedy, drawing in recordings that caught the embodiment of cat beguile. TikTok's notoriety among more youthful crowds added to the continuous development of feline recordings in the advanced scene.

3. **Livestreaming and Virtual Feline Bistros**

The appearance of livestreaming stages opened up additional opportunities for feline substance. Virtual feline bistros, where watchers could check out watch felines progressively, acquired prominence. These livestreams gave a feeling of association and unwinding for watchers, permitting them to invest energy with felines and experience the restorative advantages of cat friendship practically.

VI. Images, Remixes, and Social Effect

1. Images: Feline Recordings as Social Money

The social effect of viral feline recordings reaches out past basic diversion. Images got from these recordings, for example, the universal "I Can Has Cheezburger?" image, have become social cash. The language of feline images, frequently including hilarious subtitles and engaging articulations, fills in as a common type of correspondence inside web-based networks.

2. Remix Culture: Nyan Feline and Then some

Certain viral feline recordings, like Nyan Feline, have risen above their unique setting to become images of remix culture. Remixes, satires, and transformations of these recordings multiply across the web, exhibiting the cooperative and participatory nature of online substance creation. Nyan Feline's persevering through prominence and effect on web culture embody the peculiarity of remixes inside the viral feline video class.

VII. Moral Contemplations: The Prosperity of Cat Stars

1. Creature Government assistance and Mindful Filmmaking

As the notoriety of viral feline recordings keeps on taking off, worries about the moral treatment and prosperity of the cat-like stars have come to the front. Inquiries concerning pressure during shooting, the effect of notoriety on the existences of these creatures, and the obligation of makers to focus on the government assistance of their catlike subjects have incited conversations inside web-based networks and among creature government assistance advocates.

2. Adjusting Diversion and Feline Solace

Makers of viral feline substance face the test of finding some kind of harmony between making engaging recordings and guaranteeing the solace and prosperity of their catlike stars. Mindful filmmaking includes understanding cat conduct, keeping away from circumstances that might cause trouble, and giving a safe and supporting climate for the felines to flourish.

VIII. The Fate of Viral Feline Recordings: Patterns and Advancements

1. **Progressions in Innovation: AR and Computer generated Reality**

   As innovation keeps on propelling, the eventual fate of viral feline recordings might include vivid encounters through expanded reality (AR) and computer generated reality (VR). Watchers could wind up associating with virtual felines, encountering their fun loving shenanigans in three-layered spaces, and, surprisingly, partaking in virtual undertakings close by their #1 cat stars.

2. **Intuitive and Client Produced Content**

   The advancing scene of feline recordings might see an expanded accentuation on intelligent and client produced content. Stages could acquaint highlights that permit watchers with effectively take part in the production of feline substance, from picking the story heading of recordings to contributing components to virtual feline experiences. The obscuring of limits among makers and crowds could reclassify the elements of feline substance creation.

3. **Worldwide Coordinated efforts and Diverse Impacts**

The worldwide idea of the web considers diverse joint efforts and impacts inside the viral feline video kind. Felines from various regions of the planet could team up on virtual undertakings, and makers might draw motivation according to different social points of view to make connecting with and interesting substance. The combination of worldwide impacts could advance the narrating and variety inside the universe of viral feline recordings.

3

Chapter 3

Cats in Advertising And Marketing

In the always developing scene of publicizing and showcasing, one magnetic and all around darling animal has reliably gotten everyone's attention — the feline. From TV ads to print commercials and advanced crusades, felines have arisen as convincing envoys for items and brands. This investigation digs into the peculiarity of felines in promoting and showcasing, looking at the variables behind their adequacy, notable models, social impacts, moral contemplations, and the persevering through bid that makes cat buddies the dears of the publicizing scene.

1. **The Appeal of Cat Allure in Publicizing**
1. **Comprehensiveness and Appeal**
   Felines have an exceptional mix of appeal and appeal that rises above social and segment limits. Whether relaxing on a sun-doused windowsill or taking part in energetic tricks, felines encapsulate a comprehensiveness that reverberates with crowds around the world. This appeal fills in as a useful asset in publicizing,

making a prompt association among purchasers and the brands addressed by these charming cat figures.

2. **Profound Allure and Friendship**

The profound allure of felines in promoting lies in their capacity to bring out a large number of feelings, from happiness and entertainment to warmth and wistfulness. The friendship that felines represent hits home for watchers, taking advantage of feelings related with solace, dedication, and the delight of shared minutes. This profound reverberation improves the memorability of promotions and cultivates a positive relationship with the included items or brands.

3. **Vital and Shareable Substance**

Felines innately loan themselves to making noteworthy and shareable substance. The capriciousness of cat conduct, combined with their attractive characteristics, brings about outwardly captivating and frequently diverting promotions. In the time of virtual entertainment, where shareability is a critical measurement of progress, feline driven promotions can possibly become a web sensation, contacting immense crowds and expanding the span of showcasing efforts a long ways past their underlying openness.

II. Famous Models: Felines Capturing everyone's attention in Commercials

1. **Morris the Feline: 9 Lives and then some**

One of the earliest and most notable instances of a feline in promoting is Morris the Feline, the fussy cat mascot for 9Lives feline food. Appearing during the 1960s, Morris turned into a commonly recognized name and an image of knowing taste. His modern yet lively persona reverberated with crowds, making him a dearest and persevering through figure in the realm of feline driven showcasing.

2. **The Cheshire Feline and Alice in Wonderland**

   The Cheshire Feline from Lewis Carroll's "Alice's Experiences in Wonderland" has risen above writing to turn into a getting through image in promoting and mainstream society. With its cryptic smile and eccentric attitude, the Cheshire Feline has been highlighted in different commercials, from elevating items connected with the adored story to epitomizing the slippery and secretive characteristics that advertisers try to summon in their missions.

3. **The Friskies Impact: Feline Food Goes Computerized**

   In the computerized age, brands like Friskies have utilized the web's adoration for feline substance to make connecting with and engaging notices. The "Dear Cat" series, created by Friskies, includes a shrewd and experienced feline giving funny counsel to another cat. The outcome of this mission shows the viability of utilizing narrating and go along with to interface with crowds on an individual level.

4. **Catvertising: EHarmony's Feline Woman**

EHarmony's "Feline Woman" business adopted an entertaining strategy to interface with its crowd. The promotion includes a lady who, as she continued looking for affection, communicates a mind-boggling partiality for felines. The flippant depiction resounded with watchers, turning into a viral sensation and displaying the force of humor and appeal in making essential ads.

III. Social Impacts: Felines as Social Images in Advertising

1. **Japanese Feline Culture: Hi Kitty and Then some**

   In Japan, felines hold a unique spot in social and stylish customs. Hi Kitty, an internationally perceived character made by Sanrio, epitomizes the crossing point of felines and promoting. The feline molded character has turned into a social peculiarity, enhancing a large number of items and rising above age and orientation socioeconomics. Past Welcome Kitty, the Maneki-neko, or enticing feline, is a customary image of best of luck and thriving, frequently integrated into showcasing efforts to convey positive relationship with items.

2. **Web Culture: Feline Images and Online Patterns**

The web plays had a huge impact in hoisting felines to the situation with web big names and image sensations. Testy Feline, Lil Buddy, and other cat forces to be reckoned with have become images of online culture, moving images, emoticons, and web shoptalk. Advertisers exploit these web-based patterns by integrating famous feline images into ads, making a feeling of social pertinence and interfacing with the web keen segment.

3. **Feline Bistros: Advertising Encounters and Feeling**

Feline bistros, at first promoted in Japan, have become worldwide peculiarities, consolidating the allure of felines with the experience of getting a charge out of espresso or tea in a catlike well disposed climate. Advertisers have quickly taken advantage of the chance to adjust their brands to the comfortable and encouraging climate of feline bistros, making organizations and limited time occasions that tap into the social appeal of these foundations.

IV. Moral Contemplations: Adjusting Double-dealing and Legitimacy

1. **Capable Creature Portrayal**

The utilization of creatures in promoting raises moral contemplations in regards to their prosperity and treatment. Capable advertisers focus on the government assistance of creatures highlighted in commercials, guaranteeing that they are treated with care, not exposed to unjustifiable pressure, and furnished with a protected climate. The accentuation is on valid and conscious portrayal that lines up with moral norms and advances a positive picture for the brand.

2. **Keeping away from Generalizations and Abuse**

   Advertisers should explore the scarcely discernible difference between utilizing the allure of felines and staying away from generalizations or double-dealing. Cliché depictions, for example, giving felines a role as simply decorative or involving them as props without thought for their prosperity, can prompt reaction from buyers and creature government assistance advocates. Legitimacy and capable portrayal are significant in building a positive brand picture.

3. **Adjusting Diversion and Moral Practices**

The test lies in adjusting the diversion worth of feline driven promoting with moral practices. While comical or eccentric depictions of felines can be engaging, advertisers should guarantee that the prosperity of the creatures outweighs everything else. Straightforward correspondence about the treatment of creatures in the background encourages entrust with shoppers and upgrades the validity of the brand.

V. The Developing Scene: Felines in Computerized Promoting and Online Entertainment

1. **Virtual Entertainment and Feline Powerhouses**

   The coming of virtual entertainment has led to another variety of cat powerhouses — felines with committed followings on stages like Instagram and TikTok. Advertisers progressively team up with feline powerhouses to use their prominence and draw in with crowds in a bona fide and natural way. The visual idea of online entertainment adjusts consistently with the attractive characteristics of felines, setting out open doors for brands to feature items in outwardly engaging and shareable ways.

2. **Client Produced Content and Challenges**

   Client produced content (UGC) has turned into a useful asset in computerized showcasing, and felines assume a focal part in this pattern. Brands urge customers to share photographs and recordings of their felines communicating with items, making a feeling of local area and cooperation. Challenges revolved around feline related topics produce drawing in happy as well as cultivate a feeling of brand devotion among members.

3. Feline Channels and Expanded Reality (AR)

The joining of feline channels and expanded reality highlights in web-based entertainment stages adds a perky aspect to computerized showcasing. Brands can make intelligent encounters that permit clients to draw in with felines through channels and AR components practically. This inventive methodology upgrades client commitment and lines up with the pattern of integrating innovation into showcasing procedures.

VI. The Catvertising Upset: Patterns and Developments

1. **Reconciliation of Felines in Marking and Bundling**
   The reconciliation of felines in marking and bundling configuration has turned into a pervasive pattern. Brands influence feline symbolism to convey characteristics like perkiness, solace, or polish, adjusting the catlike tasteful to the ideal brand picture. This approach stretches out past the pet business, with felines becoming notorious images for items going from snacks to family merchandise.

2. **Personalization and Feline Driven Missions**
   Personalization is a critical technique in present day showcasing, and feline driven crusades offer a customized touch that reverberates with feline darlings. Brands make crusades that praise the remarkable characteristics of felines, permitting customers to feel seen and comprehended.
   Whether through customized informing, restrictive feline themed items, or intuitive encounters, feline driven crusades tap into the profound association among buyers and their catlike friends.

3. **Wistfulness and Feline Injected Legacies**

Wistfulness is an amazing asset in promoting, and marks gain by the immortal allure of felines by implanting returns with cat beguile. Whether reconsidering exemplary promotions with feline heroes or integrating retro feline style into contemporary missions, advertisers influence wistfulness to bring out certain feelings and make a feeling of commonality.

VII. The Persevering through Allure: Felines as Immortal Showcasing Resources

1. **Felines as Evergreen Images**
   Felines have shown to be evergreen images in advertising, holding their allure across ages. Their ageless characteristics, including effortlessness, autonomy, and liveliness, make them adaptable resources for brands trying to lay out persevering through associations with shoppers. The getting through fame of feline driven promoting grandstands the life span of the catlike bid in the always changing scene of purchaser inclinations.

2. **Close to home Reverberation and Brand Reliability**
   The profound reverberation that felines summon in publicizing adds to the development of brand unwaveringness. Customers who structure positive relationship with feline driven crusades are bound to foster a profound association with the brand. This association goes past practical parts of items, encouraging a feeling of devotion that can convert into long haul client connections.

3. **Versatility in Showcasing Systems**

Felines' versatility, deftness, and different characters make them fitting images for brands across different enterprises. From extravagance items to ordinary family things, felines consistently incorporate into promoting methodologies, bringing a bit of appeal and appeal to different shopper socioeconomics. This flexibility highlights the catlike allure's capacity to rise above unambiguous market portions.

3.1 The Use of Cats in Advertising Campaigns

In the powerful universe of promoting, where catching consideration and making enduring impressions are fundamental, one animal has reliably demonstrated to be an unrivaled resource — the feline. Cat friends, with their appeal, magnetism, and widespread allure, have become highlighted stars in a heap of publicizing efforts across different enterprises.

This exhaustive investigation dives into the murmur suasive force of felines in publicizing, looking at the variables behind their viability, notable models, social impacts, moral contemplations, and the getting through charm that makes felines the sweethearts of the showcasing scene.

1. **The Appeal of Cat Charm in Promoting**
1. **Comprehensiveness and Appeal**
   Felines have a remarkable blend of appeal and appeal that rises above social and segment limits. Their ways of behaving, articulations, and unmistakable characters make them all around engaging. Whether they're relaxing nimbly or taking part in perky jokes, felines have a natural capacity to interface with crowds on a profound, close to home level. In publicizing, this comprehensiveness and appeal act as a useful asset, making a prompt association among buyers and the brands addressed by these charming cat figures.

2. **Close to home Allure and Friendship**
   The close to home allure of felines in promoting is established in the friendship they represent. Felines, with their free yet tender nature, inspire opinions of solace, warmth, and satisfaction. Integrating felines into publicizing efforts permits brands to take advantage of these feelings, making a good relationship with their items or administrations. Watchers frequently subliminally interface the publicized brand with the good sentiments inspired by the presence of felines, encouraging a feeling of association and unwaveringness.

3. Important and Shareable Substance

Felines innately loan themselves to making vital and shareable substance. The eccentricism of cat conduct, combined with their attractive characteristics, brings about outwardly captivating and frequently clever notices. In the period of online entertainment, where shareability is a critical measurement of progress, feline driven promotions can possibly become a web sensation, contacting tremendous crowds and broadening the span of showcasing efforts a long ways past their underlying openness. The shareability of feline substance enhances brand perceivability as well as transforms watchers into dynamic members in the publicizing experience.

II. Notable Models: Cat Stars Capturing everyone's attention

1. **Morris the Feline: A Catlike Food Expert**
   One of the earliest and most notable cat stars in promoting is Morris the Feline, the insightful mascot for 9Lives feline food. Appearing during the 1960s, Morris turned into an easily recognized name and an image of cat complexity.
   His personality, typifying a feline with knowing taste, advanced the item as well as laid out an enduring heritage as a dearest promoting symbol. Morris' prosperity displayed the potential for felines to act as brand ministers, particularly inside the pet food industry.

2. **The Cheshire Feline and Wonderland Undertakings**
   The Cheshire Feline, a person from Lewis Carroll's "Alice's Undertakings in Wonderland," has risen above writing to turn into a persevering through image in publicizing and promoting. The perplexing smile and eccentric disposition of the Cheshire Feline make it a convincing figure to convey subtle characteristics or make a demeanor of secret in promoting efforts. The utilization of this famous cat in different settings features the ageless allure of felines in passing on nuanced brand messages.

3. **Friskies' "Cherished Cat": Computerized Cat Narrating**
   Friskies, a brand having some expertise in feline food, embraced the computerized age with the "Dear Cat" series. This computerized crusade highlighted a more established, savvier feline giving clever guidance to another little cat, making an endearing story that reverberated with watchers. By utilizing narrating and humor, Friskies displayed the potential for felines as static pictures as well as powerful characters in computerized content, catching the consideration of crowds in a new and connecting way.

4. **EHarmony's "Feline Woman" Business: A Fun loving Interpretation of Generalizations**

EHarmony's "Feline Woman" business adopted a hilarious strategy by tending to the cliché picture of a lady with a mind-boggling partiality for felines. The promotion exhibited the brand's similarity matching in a cheerful and engaging way. By consolidating humor and undermining generalizations, the business turned into a viral sensation, outlining the murmur suasive force of felines in making significant and shareable substance.

III. Social Impacts: Felines as Images and Envoys

1. **Japanese Feline Culture: Hi Kitty and Maneki-neko**
   In Japanese culture, felines hold an exceptional spot as images of favorable luck, appeal, and stylish allure. Hi Kitty, made by Sanrio, has turned into a worldwide symbol addressing the convergence of felines and promoting. The Maneki-neko, or coaxing feline, is one more social image related with karma and success. Marks frequently influence these social relationship to convey positive credits and adjust their items to the appeal and allure of felines.

2. **Web Culture: Felines as Online Big names**
   The web plays had a vital impact in lifting felines to the situation with online superstars. Images, viral recordings, and web-based

entertainment have transformed individual felines into social peculiarities. Cantankerous Feline, Lil Pal, and other cat powerhouses have become images of web culture, moving emoticons, images, and web shoptalk. Advertisers influence these web-based patterns to interface with more youthful, web adroit socioeconomics who resound with the appeal of web renowned felines.

3. Feline Bistros: Mixing Cat Enchant with Shopper Experience

Feline bistros, beginning in Japan and presently a worldwide peculiarity, join the adoration for felines with the experience of getting a charge out of espresso or tea in a catlike cordial climate. Advertisers have immediately jumped all over the chance to adjust their brands to the comfortable and ameliorating mood of feline bistros. Coordinated efforts, sponsorships, and special occasions in these foundations permit brands to take advantage of the social charm of feline bistros and make positive relationship with their items.

IV. Moral Contemplations: Offsetting Charm with Liability

1. **Dependable Creature Portrayal**
   The utilization of creatures in promoting, including felines, raises moral contemplations with respect to their prosperity and treatment. Dependable advertisers focus on the government assistance of creatures highlighted in commercials, guaranteeing that they are treated with care, not exposed to excessive pressure, and furnished with a protected climate. Straightforward correspondence about the treatment of creatures in the background encourages entrust with shoppers and upgrades the believability of the brand.

2. **Keeping away from Generalizations and Abuse**
   Advertisers should explore the scarcely discernible difference between utilizing the allure of felines and staying away from generalizations or abuse. Cliché depictions, for example, giving felines a role as simply fancy or involving them as props without thought

for their prosperity, can prompt reaction from buyers and creature government assistance advocates. Realness and capable portrayal are urgent in building a positive brand picture.

3. Adjusting Diversion and Moral Practices

The test lies in adjusting the diversion worth of feline driven publicizing with moral practices. While diverting or eccentric depictions of felines can be engaging, advertisers should guarantee that the prosperity of the creatures comes first.

Mindful filmmaking includes understanding cat conduct, staying away from circumstances that might cause trouble, and giving a safe and supporting climate for the felines to flourish. Brands that focus on both diversion and moral contemplations fabricate a positive standing and resound with socially cognizant buyers.

V. The Advancing Scene: Felines in the Computerized Period of Advertising

1. **Virtual Entertainment and Feline Powerhouses**

   The coming of virtual entertainment has led to another variety of cat powerhouses — felines with devoted followings on stages like Instagram and TikTok. Advertisers progressively team up with feline powerhouses to use their ubiquity and draw in with crowds in a legitimate and natural way. The visual idea of virtual entertainment adjusts flawlessly with the naturally attractive characteristics of felines, setting out open doors for brands to grandstand items in outwardly engaging and shareable ways.

2. **Client Created Content and Challenges**

   Client created content (UGC) has turned into an incredible asset in computerized showcasing, and felines assume a focal part in this pattern. Brands urge buyers to share photographs and recordings of their felines communicating with items, making a feeling of local area and cooperation. Challenges based on feline related topics create connecting with content as well as cultivate a feeling of brand unwaveringness among members. UGC crusades profit by the close to home association that clients have with their felines, transforming them into dynamic members in the brand's account.

3. **Feline Channels and Increased Reality (AR)**

The reconciliation of feline channels and expanded reality highlights in web-based entertainment stages adds an energetic aspect to computerized promoting. Brands can make intuitive encounters that permit clients to draw in with felines through channels and AR components essentially. This imaginative methodology improves client commitment and lines up with the pattern of integrating innovation into advertising procedures. By utilizing the notoriety of AR channels highlighting felines, brands can make paramount and shareable encounters that reverberate with educated purchasers.

VI. The Catvertising Transformation: Patterns and Developments

1. **Coordination of Felines in Marking and Bundling**
   The coordination of felines in marking and bundling configuration has turned into a pervasive pattern. Brands influence feline symbolism to convey characteristics like fun loving nature, solace, or polish, adjusting the catlike stylish to the ideal brand picture. This approach stretches out past the pet business, with felines becoming famous images for items going from snacks to family merchandise. Coordinating felines into marking improves visual allure and makes a close to home association with shoppers.

2. **Personalization and Feline Driven Missions**
   Personalization is a critical system in current promoting, and feline driven crusades offer a customized touch that reverberates with feline darlings. Brands make crusades that commend the novel characteristics of felines, permitting shoppers to feel seen and comprehended. Whether through customized informing,

selective feline themed items, or intelligent encounters, feline driven crusades tap into the close to home association among buyers and their catlike colleagues. Customized crusades go past nonexclusive publicizing, encouraging a feeling of individual association that fortifies brand dedication.

3. **Wistfulness and Feline Mixed Legacies**

Wistfulness is an amazing asset in showcasing, and brands benefit from the immortal allure of felines by mixing returns with cat fascinate. Whether rethinking exemplary promotions with feline heroes or integrating retro feline style into contemporary missions, advertisers influence wistfulness to inspire positive feelings and make a feeling of commonality. By taking advantage of the sentimentality related with felines, brands make a scaffold between the over a significant time span, drawing in purchasers through a common love for immortal cat fascinate.

VII. The Getting through Allure: Felines as Ageless Promoting Resources

1. **Felines as Evergreen Images**
   Felines have demonstrated to be evergreen images in promoting, holding their allure across ages. Their immortal characteristics, including effortlessness, freedom, and perkiness, make them flexible resources for brands looking to lay out getting through associations with shoppers. The getting through notoriety of feline driven promoting features the life span of the catlike claim in the consistently changing scene of shopper inclinations.

2. **Profound Reverberation and Brand Unwaveringness**
   The close to home reverberation that felines summon in publicizing adds to the development of brand reliability. Purchasers who structure positive relationship with feline driven crusades are bound to foster a profound association with the brand. This association goes past practical parts of items, encouraging

a feeling of dedication that can convert into long haul client connections. The profound bond made through feline driven publicizing turns into a main impetus in shopper navigation, impacting inclinations and decisions.

3. Flexibility in Promoting Methodologies

Felines' versatility, deftness, and different characters make them fitting images for brands across different businesses. From extravagance items to ordinary family things, felines flawlessly incorporate into promoting techniques, bringing a bit of appeal and appeal to different shopper socioeconomics. This flexibility highlights the catlike allure's capacity to rise above unambiguous market fragments, situating felines as adaptable and immortal promoting resources.

3.2 Catvertising: How Feline Faces Sell Products

In the consistently developing scene of promoting, where consideration is a valuable ware and customer commitment is a definitive objective, an astounding and wonderful pattern has arisen — catvertising. The coordination of cat countenances and characters into promoting efforts has demonstrated to be an intense and murmur suasive methodology for catching the hearts and wallets of purchasers. This exhaustive investigation digs into the universe of catvertising, unwinding the elements behind its viability, notable models, social impacts, moral contemplations, and the getting through appeal that makes felines the catlike stars of the promoting domain.

1. The Catlike Charm in Publicizing: A Widespread Moxy

1. The Puzzling Allure of Felines

Felines, with their puzzling and beguiling disposition, have a general allure that rises above social and segment limits. Their effortless developments, expressive eyes, and perky shenanigans bring out a scope of feelings, from bliss and entertainment to solace and sentimentality. Integrating felines into publicizing takes advantage of this common love for cat buddies, making a quick and close to home association among customers and the brands they address.

2. **Profound Reverberation and Friendship**

At the center of catvertising lies the close to home reverberation that felines bring out. The friendship, warmth, and euphoria related with cat presence inspire an emotional response from crowds. Whether depicted as fun loving little cats, majestic cat blue-bloods, or devilish agitators, felines become interesting characters that improve the profound allure of promoting efforts. This close to home reverberation makes a strong relationship between the promoted item and good sentiments, encouraging a feeling of association and unwaveringness among purchasers.

3. **Vital and Shareable Substance**

Felines innately loan themselves to making noteworthy and shareable substance. The eccentricism of their way of behaving, combined with their naturally attractive characteristics, brings about outwardly captivating and frequently comical commercials. In the time of virtual entertainment, where shareability is a vital measurement of progress, catvertising can possibly become a web sensation, contacting immense crowds and broadening the range of showcasing efforts a long ways past their underlying openness. The shareability of feline substance enhances brand perceivability as well as transforms watchers into dynamic members in the promoting experience.

II. Notorious Models: Cat Faces that Captured everyone's attention

1. **Morris the Feline: A Catlike Food Epicurean**

One of the earliest and most notorious instances of catvertising is Morris the Feline, the modern and knowing mascot for 9Lives feline food. Appearing during the 1960s, Morris turned into a commonly recognized name and an image of cat taste and polish. His personality advanced the item as well as laid out an enduring heritage as a dearest promoting symbol. Morris displayed the potential for felines to act as brand ministers, particularly inside the pet food industry.

2. **The Cheshire Feline and Wonderland Experiences**

   The Cheshire Feline, beginning from Lewis Carroll's "Alice's Experiences in Wonderland," has risen above writing to turn into a persevering through image in publicizing and showcasing. The perplexing smile and unusual disposition of the Cheshire Feline make it a convincing figure to convey slippery characteristics or make a quality of secret in publicizing efforts. The utilization of this notable cat in different settings grandstands the ageless allure of felines in passing on nuanced brand messages.

3. **Friskies' "Cherished Cat": Computerized Cat Narrating**

   Friskies, a brand gaining practical experience in feline food, embraced the computerized age with the "Dear Cat" series. This computerized crusade highlighted a more established, savvier feline giving comical counsel to another little cat, making an endearing story that resounded with watchers. By utilizing narrating and humor, Friskies exhibited the potential for felines as static pictures as well as powerful characters in computerized content, catching the consideration of crowds in a new and connecting way.

4. **EHarmony's "Feline Woman" Business: A Perky Interpretation of Generalizations**

EHarmony's "Feline Woman" business adopted a hilarious strategy by tending to the cliché picture of a lady with a staggering fondness for felines. The promotion exhibited the brand's similarity matching in a carefree and engaging way. By consolidating humor and undermining generalizations, the business turned into a viral sensation, showing the murmur suasive force of felines in making vital and shareable substance.

III. Social Impacts: Felines as Images and Diplomats

1. **Japanese Feline Culture: Hi Kitty and Maneki-neko**
   In Japanese culture, felines hold an extraordinary spot as images of favorable luck, appeal, and stylish allure. Hi Kitty, made by Sanrio, has turned into a worldwide symbol addressing the convergence of felines and promoting. The Maneki-neko, or enticing feline, is one more social image related with karma and flourishing. Marks frequently influence these social relationship to convey positive ascribes and adjust their items to the appeal and allure of felines.

2. **Web Culture: Felines as Online Superstars**
   The web plays had a urgent impact in raising felines to the situation with online VIPs. Images, viral recordings, and online entertainment have transformed individual felines into social peculiarities. Cantankerous Feline, Lil Buddy, and other cat forces to be reckoned with have become images of web culture, rousing emoticons, images, and web shoptalk. Advertisers influence these web-based patterns to interface with more youthful, web insightful socioeconomics who reverberate with the appeal of web popular felines.

3. **Feline Bistros: Mixing Cat Enchant with Shopper Experience**

Feline bistros, beginning in Japan and presently a worldwide peculiarity, consolidate the affection for felines with the experience of getting a charge out of espresso or tea in a catlike cordial climate. Advertisers have jumped all over the chance to adjust their brands to the comfortable and encouraging atmosphere of feline bistros. Coordinated efforts, sponsorships, and special occasions in these foundations permit brands to take advantage of the social appeal of feline bistros and make positive relationship with their items.

IV. Moral Contemplations: Offsetting Adorableness with Obligation

1. **Capable Creature Portrayal**

   The utilization of creatures in promoting, including felines, raises moral contemplations in regards to their prosperity and treatment. Dependable advertisers focus on the government assistance of creatures highlighted in commercials, guaranteeing that they are treated with care, not exposed to excessive pressure, and furnished with a protected climate. Straightforward correspondence about the treatment of creatures in the background encourages entrust with customers and improves the believability of the brand.

2. **Keeping away from Generalizations and Abuse**

   Advertisers should explore the scarce difference between utilizing the allure of felines and staying away from generalizations or abuse.

   Cliché depictions, for example, giving felines a role as simply elaborate or involving them as props without thought for their prosperity, can prompt reaction from buyers and creature government assistance advocates. Validness and capable portrayal are vital in building a positive brand picture.

3. **Adjusting Diversion and Moral Practices**

The test lies in adjusting the diversion benefit of catvertising with moral practices. While diverting or capricious depictions of felines can be engaging, advertisers should guarantee that the prosperity of the creatures outweighs everything else. Mindful filmmaking includes understanding cat conduct, staying away from circumstances that might cause trouble, and giving a safe and sustaining climate for the felines to flourish. Brands that focus on both diversion and moral contemplations construct a positive standing and resound with socially cognizant purchasers.

V. The Advancing Scene: Felines in the Computerized Period of Promoting

1. **Online Entertainment and Feline Powerhouses**

   The coming of web-based entertainment has led to another variety of cat powerhouses — felines with committed followings on stages like Instagram and TikTok. Advertisers progressively team up with feline powerhouses to use their ubiquity and draw in with crowds in a legitimate and natural way. The visual idea of virtual entertainment adjusts flawlessly with the attractive characteristics of felines, setting out open doors for brands to exhibit items in outwardly engaging and shareable ways.

2. **Client Created Content and Challenges**

   Client created content (UGC) has turned into an integral asset in computerized promoting, and felines assume a focal part in this pattern. Brands urge customers to share photographs and recordings of their felines interfacing with items, making a feeling of local area and support. Challenges based on feline related topics produce connecting with content as well as cultivate a feeling of brand unwaveringness among members. UGC crusades exploit the close to home association that clients have with their felines, transforming them into dynamic members in the brand's story.

3. **Feline Channels and Increased Reality (AR)**

The mix of feline channels and expanded reality highlights in online entertainment stages adds a fun loving aspect to computerized showcasing. Brands can make intuitive encounters that permit clients to draw in with felines through channels and AR components essentially. This creative methodology improves client commitment and lines up with the pattern of integrating innovation into showcasing systems. By utilizing the prevalence of AR channels including felines, brands can make important and shareable encounters that resound with educated buyers.

VI. The Catvertising Upset: Patterns and Advancements

1. **Combination of Felines in Marking and Bundling**

   The combination of felines in marking and bundling configuration has turned into a predominant pattern. Brands influence feline symbolism to convey characteristics like liveliness, solace, or style, adjusting the catlike tasteful to the ideal brand picture. This approach stretches out past the pet business, with felines becoming notorious images for items going from snacks to family products. Coordinating felines into marking upgrades visual allure and makes a profound association with purchasers.

2. **Personalization and Feline Driven Missions**

   Personalization is a vital methodology in present day showcasing, and feline driven crusades offer a customized touch that resounds with feline darlings. Brands make crusades that commend the interesting characteristics of felines, permitting shoppers to feel seen and comprehended. Whether through customized informing, selective feline themed items, or intelligent encounters, feline driven crusades tap into the profound association among purchasers and their catlike friends. Customized crusades go past nonexclusive promoting, encouraging a feeling of individual association that reinforces brand dependability.

3. **Wistfulness and Feline Implanted Legacies**

Wistfulness is an incredible asset in promoting, and marks profit by the immortal allure of felines by mixing returns with cat enchant. Whether reconsidering exemplary promotions with feline heroes or integrating retro feline feel into contemporary missions, advertisers influence wistfulness to bring out good feelings and make a feeling of commonality. By taking advantage of the sentimentality related with felines, brands make an extension between the over a wide span of time, drawing in customers through a common love for immortal cat fascinate.

VII. The Getting through Allure: Felines as Immortal Showcasing Resources

1. **Felines as Evergreen Images**

   Felines have shown to be evergreen images in promoting, holding their allure across ages. Their ageless characteristics, including beauty, autonomy, and fun loving nature, make them flexible resources for brands looking to lay out getting through associations with customers. The persevering through ubiquity of feline driven publicizing features the life span of the catlike request in the steadily changing scene of buyer inclinations.

2. **Close to home Reverberation and Brand Faithfulness**

   The close to home reverberation that felines summon in publicizing adds to the development of brand dedication. Buyers who structure positive relationship with feline driven crusades are bound to foster a profound association with the brand.

   This association goes past practical parts of items, encouraging a feeling of dedication that can convert into long haul client connections. The profound bond made through feline driven publicizing turns into a main impetus in buyer navigation, impacting inclinations and decisions.

3. **Versatility in Showcasing Techniques**

Felines' versatility, deftness, and different characters make them fitting images for brands across different businesses. From extravagance items to regular family things, felines consistently coordinate into promoting techniques, bringing a dash of appeal and appeal to different buyer socioeconomics. This flexibility highlights the catlike allure's capacity to rise above unambiguous market sections, situating felines as adaptable and immortal promoting resources.

3.3 Cats as Brand Ambassadors

In the serious domain of showcasing and publicizing, where catching shopper consideration is an unending test, brands have found a flighty yet surprisingly powerful technique — utilizing the natural allure of felines as brand representatives. These mysterious cat partners, with their widespread appeal and close to home reverberation, have arisen as murmur suasive ministers fit for producing genuine associations among buyers and brands.

Felines have a remarkable mix of characteristics that make them ideal delegates for many items and administrations. Their smooth developments, expressive eyes, and perky tricks make a prompt and profound association with crowds, rising above social and segment limits. This all inclusive allure fills in as an incredible asset for brands looking to impart messages that resound on a profound, close to home level.

The close to home reverberation related with felines stretches out past simple style. Felines summon opinions of friendship, solace, and delight, encouraging positive relationship with the brands they address. Whether depicted as magnificent figures, perky cats, or devilish characters, felines become engaging brand ministers that upgrade the general allure of publicizing efforts. The profound bond fashioned through these portrayals adds to expanded brand steadfastness, as customers foster positive relationship with the items or administrations supported by their catlike ministers.

The murmur suasive force of felines as brand representatives is exemplified by notable models in publicizing history. Morris the Feline, for example, turned into an image of cat refinement and wisdom as the mascot for 9Lives feline food. Morris' persona advanced the item as well as left a getting through heritage as a darling promoting symbol. This early achievement exhibited the potential for felines to act as envoys, especially inside the pet business.

The utilization of felines as brand representatives isn't restricted to explicit item classes. The Cheshire Feline from Lewis Carroll's "Alice's Experiences in Wonderland" has risen above writing to turn into an image of subtle characteristics in different promoting efforts. The eccentric disposition and puzzling smile of the Cheshire Feline make a special and significant portrayal that lines up with the brand's informing.

In the advanced age, feline forces to be reckoned with have arisen as online famous people, further cementing the job of felines as brand envoys. Online entertainment stages like Instagram and TikTok include felines with devoted followings, and advertisers progressively team up with these catlike powerhouses to contact different and drew in crowds. The visual idea of online entertainment adjusts flawlessly with the attractive characteristics of felines, permitting brands to grandstand items in outwardly engaging and shareable ways.

The getting through allure of felines as brand representatives is established in their flexibility and adaptability. Felines consistently incorporate into different advertising methodologies, representing characteristics going from perkiness and style to autonomy and interest. This flexibility permits felines to address a wide cluster of items, from pet-related products to way of life and extravagance brands.

As brand ministers, felines likewise assume a vital part in making important and shareable substance. The flightiness of their way of behaving, joined with their effortlessly attractive characteristics, brings about outwardly captivating notices that can possibly circulate around the web. Feline driven content catches consideration as well as empowers dynamic support from watchers, transforming them into brand advocates through the demonstration of sharing.

Chapter 4

Cats in Fashion

In the realm of design, where imagination exceeds all logical limitations, felines have tracked down their place as notable and charming images. The crossing point of cat beguile and the masterfulness of design has led to a dazzling and flexible pattern that rises above time and patterns. This thorough investigation digs into the complex connection among felines and design, revealing the authentic impacts, present day understandings, and the persevering through charm that has made felines an essential piece of the style scene.

1. **Cat Tastefulness Through the Ages**
1. **Authentic Portrayals of Felines in Style**
   Felines have been related with tastefulness and beauty since the beginning of time, affecting design in unobtrusive yet huge ways. In antiquated Egypt, felines were respected and frequently portrayed in gems and articles of clothing, representing security and favorable luck. The glorious and puzzling air of cats made a permanent imprint on the design sensibilities of that time,

making way for a well established relationship among felines and extravagance.

2. Felines in Renaissance Workmanship and Imagery

The Renaissance time frame saw the ascent of imagery in workmanship, and felines became metaphorical figures in artworks, embroideries, and materials. Representing freedom and secret, felines decorated the attire and adornments of the tip top, becoming insignias of complexity and refinement. The catlike impact in Renaissance design laid the basis for the getting through relationship among felines and high culture.

II. Feline Themes in Contemporary Style

1. Runway Catwalks: Cat Motivations in High fashion

In current style, feline themes have become the dominant focal point on esteemed runways, with originators integrating cat roused components into their assortments. From feline molded gems to unconventional feline prints on pieces of clothing, the runway has turned into a jungle gym for investigating the fun loving and rich sides of feline design. Top of the line marks every now and again draw motivation from the catlike world, making pieces that commend the persona and appeal of felines.

2. Catwalk Big names: Design and Cat Forces to be reckoned with

The computerized age has seen the development of feline powerhouses via web-based entertainment stages, where cat style takes on another aspect. Felines with committed followings become style symbols by their own doing, wearing hand crafted outfits and embellishments that catch the consideration of design lovers around the world. This combination of catwalk VIPs and cat powerhouses features the contemporary interest with coordinating felines into the domain of style.

III. Feline Style in Ordinary Closets

1. **Feline Print Clothing: From Relaxed to Stylish**

   Feline prints have turned into a staple in ordinary design, enhancing an extensive variety of clothing from shirts and dresses to frill like scarves and satchels. The flexibility of feline themed clothing permits people to communicate their affection for cats in different styles, going from charming and capricious to smooth and modern. Feline prints have penetrated streetwear and easygoing style, turning into an in vogue and open method for integrating cat engage into everyday closets.

2. **Feline Embellishments: Murmur sonalizing Design Proclamations**

Embellishments assume a vital part in customizing design proclamations, and feline themed extras have become unquestionable requirements for cat fans. Feline molded gems, satchels including cat themes, and feline roused footwear add a bit of eccentricity to outfits while displaying an affection for felines. The prevalence of feline embellishments stretches out past easygoing wear, with creators injecting top of the line design with cat pizazz through painstakingly made pieces that hoist the imaginativeness of feline style.

IV. Cat Impact in Extravagance Style

1. **Cat Symbols in Extravagance Marking**

   Extravagance marks often integrate cat symbols into their marking, conforming to the ageless characteristics related with felines. From the famous Cartier jaguar to Gucci's catlike themes, extravagance style houses influence the class and persona of felines to make unmistakable and conspicuous images. The mix of cat symbolism upgrades the optimistic allure of extravagance style, connecting these brands with complexity and refinement.

2. **Joint efforts with Feline Fashioners**

The universe of style has seen joint efforts between eminent planners and feline aficionados who bring their affection for cats into the plan cycle. Feline themed container assortments and restricted version joint efforts exhibit the convergence of high style and the energetic appeal of felines.

These associations not just praise the one of a kind connection among originators and their catlike muses yet in addition add to the developing story of feline style in extravagance circles.

V. Catwalks and Short snoozes: Style Photography with Cats

1. **Felines as Photograph Shoot Buddies**
   Style photography has embraced the presence of felines as enchanting mates during photograph shoots. The juxtaposition of smooth models embellished in couture with the impulsive notion of a feline relaxing on a rich background makes outwardly convincing stories. The sincere and flighty nature of felines adds a component of immediacy to mold photography, splitting away from regular standards and implanting a feeling of perkiness.
2. **Feline Models: Cat Countenances in Style Articles**

Cat faces have graced the pages of design articles, with felines assuming the job of models by their own doing. Whether presenting close by human models or catching consideration with their striking look, felines become basic to the visual narrating of design spreads. This pattern mirrors the persevering through interest with cat class and the craving to coordinate the appeal of felines into the story of high design.

VI. Catwalks to Feline Recordings: Cat Design in Mainstream society

1. **Felines in Music Recordings and Mainstream society Symbolism**
   Past the customary catwalks of design shows, felines have influenced music recordings and mainstream society symbolism.

Specialists and originators frequently integrate cat components into their visual narrating, making a consistent mix of style and mainstream society. The predominance of feline symbolism in music recordings adds a hint of eccentricity as well as supports the boundless social allure of cats.

2. **Web Felines: From Images to Product**

The web's relationship with felines has led to another type of cat style — stock including web renowned felines. Images, viral recordings, and online characters like Irritable Feline and Lil Buddy have turned into the essences of feline driven stock, including clothing, embellishments, and way of life items. This peculiarity shows the force of web culture in molding the style of feline design and its effect on standard buyer inclinations.

VII. Moral Contemplations in Feline Design

1. **Creature Government assistance and Savagery Free Design**
As the prominence of feline style develops, moral contemplations with respect to creature government assistance and remorselessness free practices come to the front.
Dependable shoppers and architects focus on the utilization of reasonable materials and moral creation strategies to guarantee that no damage comes to creatures in the making of feline themed design things. The shift towards brutality free design mirrors a more extensive consciousness of moral worries inside the style business.

2. **The Ascent of Vegetarian Feline Design**

Because of moral worries, the design business has seen the development of veggie lover feline style — items that celebrate cat feel without utilizing creature inferred materials. Veggie lover calfskin, false fur, and other mercilessness free choices have become indispensable to feline motivated design, furnishing cognizant shoppers with classy choices that line up with their qualities. The ascent of veggie lover feline style connotes a positive shift towards additional manageable and merciful decisions inside the business.

4.1 The Influence of Cats in Fashion Design

In the dynamic and always advancing universe of style configuration, felines have arisen as notorious dreams, motivating fashioners to mesh cat class and eccentricity into their manifestations. This broad investigation digs into the significant impact of felines on style configuration, following the verifiable roots, looking at contemporary articulations, and revealing the bunch manners by which these puzzling animals have left their permanent paw prints on the runway.

1. **Verifiable Roots: Felines as Images of Tastefulness**
1. **Old Egypt: Cat Gods and Embellishments**

   The interest with felines in design tracks down its underlying foundations in old Egypt, where these majestic animals were venerated as images of security and beauty. Felines were related with divinities like Bastet, the goddess of home, fruitfulness, and assurance. Egyptians enhanced themselves with feline themed gems, pieces of clothing, and extras, conveying a feeling of complexity and heavenly association. The effortless stance of felines and their baffling atmosphere made a getting through imprint on the tasteful sensibilities of the time.

2. **Renaissance Purposeful anecdotes: Felines as Metaphorical Figures**

The Renaissance time frame saw the resurgence of imagery in craftsmanship and design. Felines became metaphorical figures, representing freedom, secret, and refinement. Artistic creations and embroideries included felines as allies to privileged figures, featuring their relationship with high culture and complexity. The unpretentious consolidation of cat themes into attire and extras during the Renaissance set up for the getting through charm of felines in style.

II. The Catwalk Annals: Cat Motivations on Runways

1. Runway Sovereignty: Feline Themes in High fashion

In the advanced period, feline themes have graced the runways of regarded style houses, with creators embracing cat motivations in high fashion. From feline formed adornments to many-sided feline prints on lavish textures, fashioners commend the persona and style of felines. Top of the line marks frequently draw on the imagery of felines to make remarkable and conspicuous pieces that hoist the imaginativeness of style.

2. Cat Appearances on the Catwalk: Models and Dream

The catwalk has seen feline themes as well as live cat models swaggering close by human models. Originators have brought felines into runway shows, injecting a component of flightiness and perkiness. These catlike models become muses, spellbinding crowds and adding a hint of eccentricity to the conventional catwalk experience. The combination of cat tastefulness with human design makes an enamoring visual story.

III. Regular Polish: Feline Design in Closets

1. Feline Prints: Easygoing to Couture

Feline prints have changed from relaxed wear to high fashion, turning into a flexible and famous decision in regular style. Shirts, dresses, and embellishments enhanced with unusual feline prints permit people to communicate their affection for cats in different styles. Originators and standard style brands embrace feline prints as an energetic and open method for injecting closets with the appeal of felines. The universality of feline prints mirrors the expansive allure of cat style.

2. Feline Frill: A Murmur sonal Contact

Frill assume a urgent part in customizing style explanations, and feline themed embellishments have become sought after things for cat fans. Feline formed gems, satchels including cat themes, and feline motivated footwear permit people to add an inconspicuous or striking dash of cat tastefulness to their outfits. The notoriety of feline extras reaches out past relaxed wear, with creators making very good quality pieces that feature the creativity of feline enlivened style.

IV. Extravagance Feline Stylish: Cat Symbols in Top of the line Design

1. **Notable Images: Felines in Extravagance Marking**
   Extravagance style houses have integrated cat symbols into their marking, making ageless and conspicuous images. The Cartier puma and Gucci's catlike themes are model of how top of the line brands influence the style and persona of felines to convey complexity and refinement. Cat symbolism turns into an essential piece of extravagance style, adding a bit of selectiveness and optimistic charm.

2. **Cooperation Couture: Fashioners and Cat Aficionados**

The coordinated effort among creators and cat aficionados has led to novel and restricted release assortments that commend the connection among people and their catlike buddies. Feline themed container assortments, frequently including the plans of feline sweethearts, grandstand the crossing point of high design and individual enthusiasm. These coordinated efforts raise feline style as well as highlight the close to home association among fashioners and their catlike muses.

V. Cat Presence in Design Photography

1. **Feline Upgraded Visual Narrating**
   Design photography has embraced the presence of felines as beguiling sidekicks during photograph shoots. The juxtaposition of smooth models enhanced in couture with the fanciful notion of a feline relaxing on sumptuous sceneries makes outwardly convincing stories. Felines improve the narrating part of style

photography, adding a component of validness and capriciousness to painstakingly organized pictures.

2. Feline Models: Cat Countenances in Article Spreads

Cat faces have graced the pages of design publications, with felines assuming the job of models close by human partners. Whether presenting with style or catching consideration with their striking look, felines become indispensable to the visual narrating of design spreads. This pattern mirrors the getting through interest with cat style and the craving to coordinate the appeal of felines into the account of high design.

VI. Catwalks to Feline Recordings: Cat Design in Mainstream society

1. Felines in Music Recordings and Mainstream society Symbolism

Past customary catwalks, cat design has saturated music recordings and mainstream society symbolism. Specialists and originators frequently integrate cat components into their visual narrating, making a consistent mix of design and mainstream society. The pervasiveness of feline symbolism in music recordings adds a bit of eccentricity and supports the boundless social allure of cats.

2. Web Felines: From Images to Product

The web's relationship with felines has led to another type of cat style — stock highlighting web popular felines. Images, viral recordings, and online characters like Grouchy Feline and Lil Pal have turned into the essences of feline driven stock, including attire, adornments, and way of life items. This peculiarity shows the force of web culture in forming the feel of feline style and its effect on standard shopper inclinations.

VII. Moral Contemplations in Feline Style Plan

1. Creature Government assistance and Dependable Plan

The developing familiarity with moral contemplations in style configuration has provoked a shift toward additional capable and economical practices. Architects and customers the same supporter for creature government assistance, prompting expanded utilization of savagery free materials in feline themed style. Moral contemplations additionally stretch out to creation strategies, with an accentuation on straightforward and capable plan rehearses that focus on the prosperity of creatures.

2. Vegetarian Feline Style: Mercilessness Free Tastefulness

In light of moral worries, the style business has seen the ascent of vegetarian feline design — items that celebrate cat feel without utilizing creature determined materials. Veggie lover cowhide, artificial fur, and other mercilessness free choices have become indispensable to feline roused design, furnishing cognizant shoppers with sharp choices that line up with their qualities. The hug of vegetarian feline design connotes a positive shift towards additional supportable and humane decisions inside the business.

VIII. The Catlike Eventual fate of Style Plan

1. Catwalks and Innovativeness: Persevering through Motivations

The impact of felines in style configuration gives no indications of disappearing. As originators keep on drawing motivation from the class, secret, and energy of felines, cat themes will probably continue on runways, in regular wear, and in very good quality style marking. The getting through allure of felines as dreams mirrors their immortal characteristics, making them an enduring wellspring of inventive motivation for the design business.

2. Inclusivity in Cat Style: A Murmur spective Shift

Cat design can possibly develop towards more prominent inclusivity, embracing a different scope of feline varieties and articulations.

Fashioners might investigate one of a kind examples, tones, and styles that commend the extravagance of cat variety.

This inclusivity could stretch out to joint efforts with feline salvage associations and missions advancing the prosperity of felines, encouraging a positive and socially capable aspect to cat roused design.

4.2 Catwalk Cats: Feline Inspirations in Fashion Shows

Style, with its steadily spinning pattern of patterns and impacts, has a well established love illicit relationship with cat class. Felines, with their effortlessness, secret, and energy, play rose above their parts as family allies to become notable motivations for fashioners on the world's most esteemed catwalks. This thorough investigation digs into the captivating universe of "Catwalk Felines," following the authentic roots, looking at contemporary articulations, and uncovering the bunch manners by which cat motivations have made a permanent imprint on the runway.

1. **The Authentic Tastefulness of Felines in Style**
1. **Old Egypt: Cat Eminence on the Nile**
   The authentic association among felines and design tracks down its underlying foundations in antiquated Egypt, where these baffling animals were respected as images of security, beauty, and heavenly nature. Egyptians enhanced themselves with feline enlivened adornments and articles of clothing, adjusting their clothing to the greatness related with cats. The mysterious charm of felines in old Egyptian design established the groundwork for the persevering through relationship among felines and tastefulness.
2. **Renaissance Purposeful anecdotes: Felines as Images of Respectability**

The Renaissance time frame saw a resurgence of interest in imagery, and felines became metaphorical figures in compositions and materials. Representing freedom, secret, and honorability, felines enhanced the apparel and adornments of the world class. The unpretentious joining of cat themes into Renaissance design denoted a continuation of the immortal association among felines and high culture.

II. Cat Thrive on Contemporary Catwalks

1. **The Ascent of Feline Themes in High fashion**

   In the advanced period, feline themes have climbed to conspicuousness on the catwalks of high fashion. Eminent creators draw motivation from cat polish, consolidating feline molded gems, eccentric feline prints, and, surprisingly, live cat models into their assortments. The mixture of feline themes adds a dash of perkiness and complexity to the intricate manifestations that elegance the catwalks of esteemed style houses.

2. **Live Feline Models: Swaggering Tastefulness on the Runway**

The contemporary catwalk has seen the mix of live feline models close by human partners. Planners, looking to mix unconventionality and appeal into their shows, have presented felines as style models. These catlike models enamor crowds, adding a component of eccentricity and legitimacy to the fastidiously arranged runway introductions. The juxtaposition of smooth, couture-clad models with the normal polish of felines makes an enrapturing visual display.

III. Catwalk Big names: Cat Forces to be reckoned with in the Style Business

1. **Catwalk Eminence: Cat Forces to be reckoned with via Online Entertainment**

   In the advanced age, felines have climbed to the situation with powerhouses via virtual entertainment stages. Instagram, specifically, has turned into a virtual catwalk for cat superstars with devoted followings. These feline powerhouses, enhanced in uniquely designed outfits and embellishments, exhibit the convergence of cat polish and high style. Creators and brands team up with these catwalk VIPs to contact drew in and different crowds, further hardening the impact of felines in the design business.

2. Chic: Felines as Pioneers in Web-based Culture

Felines have become trailblazers in web-based culture, affecting style and moving catwalk-commendable looks. Images, viral recordings, and web well known felines have become social peculiarities, molding the style of feline motivated design. The web's reverence of felines has moved them into the spotlight as powerful figures in the always advancing scene of style and mainstream society.

IV. From Catwalks to Feline Recordings: Cat Style in Mainstream society

1. **Cat Design in Music Recordings and Promotion Missions**
   The appeal of cat tastefulness stretches out past conventional catwalks to saturate music recordings and promoting efforts. Specialists and brands influence feline symbolism to add a hint of eccentricity, complexity, or secret to visual narrating. Whether highlighted in music recordings or as conspicuous figures in promoting, felines add to the combination of design and mainstream society, cementing their job as compelling dreams in the imaginative business.

2. **Marketing the Catwalk: Felines as Brand Ministers**

The web's interest with felines has led to another type of cat style — stock including web renowned felines. Images, viral recordings, and online characters like Testy Feline and Lil Pal have turned into the essences of feline driven stock. From attire and accomplices to way of life items, felines act as brand diplomats, making an interpretation of their internet based impact into substantial articulations of cat propelled style.

V. The Imaginativeness of Catwalk Plan: Cat Themes and Couture Craftsmanship

1. **Catwalk Couture: Style in Plan**
   Creators mix catwalk assortments with fastidious craftsmanship, hoisting cat themes to the domain of couture. From complicatedly planned feline formed gems to pieces of clothing including hand-weaved feline prints, the creativity of catwalk plan exhibits the consistent joining of cat motivation into high design. The meticulousness and obligation to tastefulness in plan add to the persevering through allure of felines on the catwalk.

2. **Catwalk Topics: Investigating Cat Feel**

Catwalk topics frequently investigate the rich style of cat class. Fashioners draw motivation from the assorted attributes of felines — be it their agile developments, smooth fur designs, or perplexing articulations. Catwalk assortments become topical articulations of cat engage, permitting planners to praise the multi-layered appeal of felines and make an interpretation of it into wearable workmanship.

VI. Moral Contemplations in Catwalk Plan: The Empathetic Catwalk

1. **Moral Style: Focusing on Creature Government assistance**
   As the style business embraces moral contemplations, fashioners on the catwalk progressively focus on creature government assistance. Dependable obtaining of materials, remorselessness free style, and straightforward creation strategies have become vital to catwalk plan. The shift towards moral design mirrors a more extensive obligation to guaranteeing that the impact of felines on the catwalk lines up with standards of empathy and supportability.

2. **Vegetarian Catwalks: Brutality Free Couture**

In light of moral worries, the idea of vegetarian catwalks has arisen, highlighting plans made from mercilessness free materials. Veggie lover calfskin, fake fur, and economical options become the overwhelming focus, permitting architects to exhibit their obligation to creature well disposed style. Vegetarian catwalks address an agreeable combination of cat class and moral contemplations, rethinking the scene of high design with sympathy at its center.

VII. The Murmur spective Shift: Inclusivity and Variety on the Catwalk

1. **Comprehensive Catwalks: Observing Cat Variety**
   The developing scene of catwalks mirrors a murmur spective shift towards inclusivity. Fashioners investigate a different scope of feline varieties, examples, and articulations, praising the wealth of cat variety. Comprehensive catwalks urge originators to grandstand different styles that resound with a wide crowd, encouraging a more delegate and open way to deal with cat motivated design.

2. **Coordinated efforts with Feline Salvage Associations: A Socially Mindful Catwalk**

In a period of social obligation, catwalks progressively work together with feline salvage associations. Style shows become stages to bring issues to light about creature government assistance, advance selections, and add to the prosperity of felines. Joint efforts with salvage associations not just inject catwalks with a socially dependable aspect yet in addition feature the positive effect of the design business on cat networks.

VIII. The Fate of Catwalk Felines: Persevering through Motivations

1. **Catwalks and Innovativeness: Ageless Motivations**
   The impact of felines on catwalks is a demonstration of their immortal and persevering through bid. As creators keep on drawing motivation from the class, secret, and perkiness of felines, cat themes will probably stay fundamental to the story of high design. Catwalks will keep on being spaces where inventiveness

and cat impacts join, making remarkable minutes that spellbind crowds around the world.

2. Cat Stylish: A Proceeded with Impact

The fate of catwalk felines holds the commitment of proceeded with impact and advancement. Fashioners might investigate new roads to communicate cat style, exploring different avenues regarding materials, subjects, and coordinated efforts that push the limits of regular catwalk plan. Cat chic drives will probably prompt the investigation of strange domains, guaranteeing that the impact of felines on catwalks stays dynamic and pertinent.

4.3 The Popularity of Cat Merchandise

In the huge scene of purchaser culture, one specific specialty has ascended to unmistakable quality with astounding enthusiasm — the universe of feline product. Felines, those puzzling and beguiling friends, have become dearest pets as well as famous images that move a wide exhibit of product. This thorough investigation dives into the multi-layered domain of feline product, following its verifiable roots, analyzing the latest things, and revealing the elements that add to the persevering through fame of everything cat.

1. The Authentic Foundations of Feline Product

1. Antiquated Adoration: Felines in Imagery and Embellishments

The authentic association among felines and product traces all the way back to old civic establishments. In societies like antiquated Egypt, felines were loved and embellished with adornments, talismans, and different knickknacks as images of security, secret, and eternality.

The feline's relationship with positive credits pursued it a well known decision for individual decorations, establishing the groundwork for the getting through allure of feline product from the beginning of time.

2. Renaissance Style: Felines in Craftsmanship and Design

The Renaissance time frame saw the resurgence of interest in imagery, and felines tracked down their direction into craftsmanship and style. Artistic creations and embroideries included cat themes, and the figurative meaning of felines as images of respectability and secret stretched out to stock. From dress embellishments to extras, feline themed stock turned into an unmistakable articulation of the social interest with cat tastefulness.

II. Feline Product in the Contemporary Time

1. **The Ascent of Web Felines: Impetus for Feline Product Patterns**

   The coming of the web, especially virtual entertainment stages, denoted a groundbreaking period for feline product. Web felines, with their viral recordings, images, and devoted followings, became powerful figures in mainstream society. This web-based peculiarity essentially added to the flood popular for feline themed stock, making a worldwide local area of feline lovers anxious to communicate their catlike being a fan.

2. **From Specialty to Standard: Feline Product Enters the Standard Market**

What was once viewed as specialty has changed into standard notoriety. Feline product has saturated different business sectors, from attire and assistants to home stylistic layout and tech contraptions. The combination of feline themed things into standard retail mirrors a change in shopper inclinations and a developing appreciation for the special appeal that felines bring to different parts of day to day existence.

III. The Different Scene of Feline Product

1. **Attire and Embellishments: Feline Style Past Cat Couture**

   Feline style stretches out past the closets of felines themselves.

Feline themed clothing and extras have become style proclamations for people, going from shirts, socks, and night robe to satchels, adornments, and even footwear. The flexibility of feline product in the domain of design permits fans to communicate their adoration for felines in different styles, from unpretentious tastefulness to strong and eccentric plans.

2. **Home Style: Feline Motivated Residing Spaces**

   Feline product has advanced into the domain of home style, changing residing spaces into articulations of cat being a fan. Feline molded furnishings, toss cushions enhanced with feline prints, and wall workmanship highlighting cat themes add to the formation of feline cordial and tastefully satisfying conditions. Home style feline product permits people to imbue their own spaces with the perky and charming characteristics of felines.

3. **Tech Contraptions and Embellishments: Felines in the Advanced Age**

   In the advanced age, feline product has flawlessly coordinated into the domain of innovation. Feline themed telephone cases, PC decals, and tech extras highlighting cat plans take care of customers who try to customize their gadgets with a dash of cat energy. The convergence of felines and innovation mirrors the inescapable impact of web felines on buyer culture.

4. **Toys and Games: Fun loving Product for Cat Fans**

Feline product isn't restricted to human purchasers; it stretches out to the catlike colleagues themselves. Toys and games planned with feline themes take special care of animal people anxious to give diversion and excitement to their shaggy companions. The lively coordination of felines into pet product underscores the comprehensive idea of cat being a fan.

IV. Feline Product in Mainstream society and Diversion

1. **The Web Feline Peculiarity: Images, Viral Recordings, and Product**

   The ascent of web felines, filled by images and viral recordings, has turned into a social peculiarity with an immediate effect on stock patterns. Surly Feline, Nyan Feline, Lil Pal, and other web well known felines have turned into the essences of feline product, showing up on all that from dress and accomplices to home merchandise and collectibles. The web feline peculiarity has raised individual felines to fame as well as added to the more extensive prominence of feline product.

2. **Feline Product in Film and TV: Cat Stars on and off the Screen**

Felines have made a permanent imprint on film and TV, adding to the prevalence of feline product in media outlets. Notorious cat characters, both vivified and genuine, have roused stock lines and collectibles. From the Cheshire Feline in "Alice in Wonderland" to the enlivened cat stars of "The Aristocats," felines in amusement have become persevering through images that resound with crowds, all things considered.

V. The Matter of Feline Product: Market Patterns and Financial Effect

1. **The Feline Product Market: Development and Broadening**

   The feline product market has encountered huge development and enhancement, mirroring the wide allure of cat topics. Online stages, specialty stores, and standard retailers offer a broad scope of feline product, taking care of customers with differing tastes and inclinations. The market's extension highlights the financial effect of the notoriety of feline themed items.

2. **Forces to be reckoned with and Coordinated efforts: Feline Product in the Time of Supports**

Powerhouses, including both web renowned felines and human characters with an affection for cats, assume a vital part in advancing feline product. Joint efforts among forces to be reckoned with and brands bring about restricted release assortments, further powering buyer interest. The support of feline product by powerhouses improves the items' perceivability and makes a feeling of legitimacy that reverberates with shoppers.

VI. The Close to home Association: Why Feline Product Resounds

1. **Profound Reverberation: Felines as Images of Solace and Happiness**
   The getting through prevalence of feline product is established in the profound reverberation that felines summon. As images of solace, friendship, and euphoria, felines hold a unique spot in the hearts of lovers. Feline product permits people to communicate and commend the profound association they share with their catlike partners, making a feeling of local area among feline sweethearts.

2. **All inclusiveness of Allure: Felines Rise above Social and Segment Limits**

Felines have an all inclusive allure that rises above social and segment limits. The inborn characteristics of felines — perkiness, interest, and freedom — resound with individuals all over the planet. Feline product, with its different scope of plans and styles, takes special care of an expansive crowd, cultivating a common appreciation for the appeal and charm of cats.

VII. Moral Contemplations in Feline Product Creation

1. **Moral Obtaining and Creation: Tending to Worries in the Business**
   The flood popular for feline product has incited moral contem-

plations inside the business. Purchasers and backing bunches underscore the significance of moral obtaining, dependable creation strategies, and straightforwardness in the assembling system. The push for moral guidelines mirrors a developing familiarity with the ecological and social effect of buyer merchandise.

2. **Supportable Feline Product: Exploring Eco-Accommodating Patterns**

The call for maintainability has affected the creation of feline product, with a rising accentuation on eco-accommodating materials and practices. Feasible feline product lines up with the upsides of naturally cognizant shoppers, making a business opportunity for items that focus on both cat subjects and moral contemplations.

VIII. Feline Product as Social Peculiarity: Effect on Society

1. **Cat Articulation in Private Personality: Feline Product as Explanations**

Feline product has turned into a method for individual articulation, permitting people to integrate their adoration for felines into their own character. From attire decisions to home stylistic layout, feline product fills in as explanations that reflect parts of character, interests, and affiliations. The social meaning of feline themed items stretches out past customer products to turn out to be important for the more extensive texture of individual and social character.

2. **Feline Product and Local area Building: Encouraging Cat People group**

The fame of feline product has worked with the development of on the web and disconnected networks joined by a common love for cats. Virtual entertainment gatherings, occasions, and get-togethers based on feline product give stages to lovers to associate, share encounters, and praise their common energy. Feline product turns into an impetus for local area building, cultivating associations that reach out past the domain of customer merchandise.

IX. The Eventual fate of Feline Product: Patterns and Prospects

1. **Mechanical Headways: Expanded Reality and Intuitive Product**

   The eventual fate of feline product is probably going to observe innovative headways that upgrade the purchaser experience. Expanded reality (AR) and intelligent product might become predominant, permitting buyers to draw in with feline themed items in creative ways. Virtual attempt ons, intuitive showcases, and vivid encounters could reclassify the scene of feline product.

2. **Customization and Personalization: Fitting Feline Product to Individual Preferences**

As buyer inclinations keep on expanding, customization and personalization will probably become key patterns in feline product. Brands might offer choices for purchasers to fit items to their singular preferences, from picking explicit feline varieties for plans to integrating individual contacts. The shift towards customized feline product mirrors a craving for novel and significant articulations of cat being a fan.

Chapter 5

Cats in Literature And Art

From the confounding charm of old Egyptian feline gods to the perky underhandedness of Cheshire in Wonderland, felines have woven themselves into the texture of human imagination. This exhaustive investigation plunges profound into the immense domains of writing and craftsmanship, following the verifiable foundations of cat impact, looking at notorious cat figures, and revealing the horde manners by which felines have become abstract and creative dreams all through the ages.

1. **Felines in Antiquated Writing: Imagery and Respect**
1. **Antiquated Egypt: Bastet and the Holy Cat Association**
   The abstract and imaginative meaning of felines in old Egypt couldn't possibly be more significant. Felines, worshipped for their beauty and defensive characteristics, ended up weaved in the folklore of the time. Bastet, the feline goddess, turned into an image of home, ripeness, and insurance, impacting both composed and visual stories. Pictographs, sonnets, and figures portrayed the hallowed association among people and cats, hoisting felines to divine status.

2. **Felines in Antiquated Greece and Rome: Familiars of the Secretive**

Antiquated Greek and Roman writing frequently depicted felines as secretive and confounding animals. They were related with the moon and the powerful, every now and again showing up as familiars of witches and otherworldly creatures. Tales and stories included felines as shrewd and sly, adding to the advancing legend encompassing these enthralling creatures.

II. Felines in Archaic Writing: Imagery and Strange notions

1. **Middle age Europe: Felines as Familiars and Signs**
   Middle age European writing painted felines with a double brush — familiars to witches and conveyors of both great and terrible signs. Fables and strange notions added to the view of felines as both enchanted and baffling creatures. This duality tracked down articulation in writing, where felines became characters exemplifying the strain between the known and the unexplored world.
2. **Feline Verse: Caprice and Veneration in Refrain**

Middle age artists frequently wrote refrains that caught the fanciful notion and appeal of felines. These sonnets went from perky depictions of cat jokes to additional serious considerations on the emblematic idea of felines.

The abstract depiction of felines in verse during this time mirrored the dualistic viewpoints — once in a while naughty, in some cases worshipped.

III. Renaissance Class: Felines as Metaphorical Figures

1. **Feline Imagery in Renaissance Workmanship and Writing**
   The Renaissance period saw a resurgence of interest in imagery and moral story. Felines became metaphorical figures addressing autonomy, secret, and honorability in both workmanship and

writing. Works of art, poems, and plays highlighted felines as allies to blue-bloods, adding a layer of complexity to their visual and composed stories.

2. Abstract Felines in Shakespearean Works

William Shakespeare, the abstract monster of the Renaissance, integrated felines into his plays, imbuing them with both emblematic and comedic importance. From the clever chat of Mercutio in "Romeo and Juliet" to the conspiring jokes of witches' familiars in "Macbeth," Shakespeare used felines as unique characters that additional profundity and interest to his works.

IV. Felines in Folktales and Fantasies: Bristly Heroes

1. Puss in Boots and Other Bristly Legends

Folktales and fantasies overflow with alluring cat characters becoming the overwhelming focus. "Puss in Boots" stands apart as an exemplary model, where a cunning feline coordinates a poverty to newfound wealth change for his lord. These stories frequently portray felines as shrewd and ingenious, winding around accounts that praise the insight and appeal of these cherished animals.

2. Legends and Odd notions: Felines in Social Accounts

Felines highlight conspicuously in worldwide legends, epitomizing a horde of jobs from defenders to comedians. Odd notions encompassing felines, like their relationship with karma and fortune, became imbued in social accounts. These scholarly and oral customs formed cultural view of felines, adding to the rich embroidered artwork of cat imagery.

V. Scholarly Felines in the Cutting edge Time: Caprice and Intricacy

1. Lewis Carroll's Wonderland: The Baffling Presence of Cheshire Feline

Lewis Carroll's "Alice's Undertakings in Wonderland" presented quite possibly of the most famous abstract feline — the Cheshire Feline. With its wicked smile and confounding appearances and vanishings, the Cheshire Feline turned into an image of eccentricity and philosophical mysteries, adding a hint of intricacy to the fantastical universe of Wonderland.

2. T.S. Eliot's Functional Felines: A Tribute to Cat Unusualness

In the twentieth hundred years, T.S. Eliot praised the unconventionalities of felines in his assortment of capricious sonnets, "Old Possum's Book of Down to earth Felines." These sonnets, later adjusted into the popular melodic "Felines," investigated the different characters and ways of behaving of felines, transforming their ordinary jokes into graceful stories that resounded with perusers all over the planet.

VI. Cat Persona in Contemporary Writing

1. **Haruki Murakami's Felines: Imagery and Existentialism**
   Contemporary writing, especially underway of Haruki Murakami, has embraced the catlike persona. Felines in Murakami's books, for example, "Kafka on the Shore" and "Norwegian Wood," act as emblematic and supernatural components. Murakami winds around perplexing stories where felines become channels for investigating existential inquiries and the limits among the real world and dream.
2. **Feline Secrets and Dreamlands: Cats in Class Fiction**

Felines keep on assuming conspicuous parts in class fiction, especially in secret and dream kinds. From comfortable secrets where cat criminal investigators tackle wrongdoings to epic dreamlands where supernatural felines have extraordinary abilities, contemporary writing exhibits the persevering through allure of felines as complex characters.

VII. Felines in Workmanship: Brushstrokes of Cat Tastefulness

1. **Old Creativity: Cat Figures in Model and Compositions**
   Antiquated workmanship honored felines through models, artworks, and earthenware. In Egypt, complex feline models and canvases embellished burial places, mirroring the profound worship for these animals. The masterfulness of the time caught the elegance and majesty of felines, sustaining their picture as images of heavenliness and security.

2. **Renaissance Polish: Felines as Pictures and Images**

Renaissance specialists embraced felines as the two subjects and images in their works. Canvases, for example, Leonardo da Vinci's "Investigation of Feline Developments and Positions" and Albrecht Dürer's "The Feline and the Mouse" displayed the craftsmen's interest with cat elegance and the emblematic wealth credited to felines during this period.

VIII. Felines in Contemporary Workmanship: From Authenticity to Extract Articulations

1. **Authenticity and Impressionism: Catching Cat Substance**
   Pragmatist and Impressionist specialists of the nineteenth and twentieth hundreds of years directed their concentration toward catching the embodiment of felines in their works. Craftsmen like Édouard Manet and Pierre-Auguste Renoir made private representations of felines, while Henriette Ronner-Knip spent significant time in painting perky and homegrown scenes highlighting felines.

2. **Oddity and Then some: Catlike Subjects in Vanguard Workmanship**

The surrealists, with their propensity for the unusual and fantastical, frequently integrated felines into their cutting edge works. Salvador Dalí's "The Elephants" included a dissolving clock enhanced with a mutilated feline, adding a component of eccentricity and secret. Felines kept on being subjects in different craftsmanship developments, from dynamic expressionism to pop workmanship.

IX. Web Felines and Contemporary Workmanship: The Advanced Material

1. **Images and Viral Felines: Computerized Creative Articulations**

   The coming of the web achieved another period for felines in craftsmanship. Images and viral felines became subjects for advanced imaginative articulations, with artists, illustrators, and computerized specialists making novel understandings of web well known cats. Computerized stages filled in as a material for the worldwide local area to draw in with and celebrate felines through workmanship.

2. **Feline Craftsmanship in the Period of Online Entertainment: From Instagram to NFTs**

Online entertainment stages, especially Instagram, have become computerized displays for feline craftsmanship. Specialists and feline fans share delineations, compositions, and computerized manifestations, cultivating a dynamic web-based local area. The ascent of non-fungible tokens (NFTs) has likewise acquainted additional opportunities for specialists with adapt and exhibit their feline themed manifestations in the advanced domain.

X. Felines as Scholarly and Imaginative Motivations: An Immortal Heritage

1. **Imagery and Purposeful anecdote: Felines as Scholarly Gadgets**

   Since the beginning of time, felines have filled in as scholarly gadgets, typifying imagery, moral story, and social importance. Whether as watchmen of old burial chambers, puzzling characters in folktales, or unusual figures in current writing, felines play

played multi-layered parts that add to the profundity and lavishness of scholarly stories.

2. Cat Feel: Felines as Imaginative Motivations

As imaginative motivations, felines have graced the materials of old figures, Renaissance show-stoppers, and contemporary advanced manifestations. Specialists, enamored by the polish and persona of felines, have looked to catch their pith through different imaginative developments, styles, and mediums, making an assorted and persevering through tradition of cat feel.

5.1 Cats as Literary Characters: Garfield, Cheshire Cat, and More

Felines, with their secretive charm, perky jokes, and free nature, have tracked down an extraordinary spot in writing all through the ages. This broad investigation digs into the universe of felines as scholarly characters, zeroing in on notorious figures, for example, Garfield, the Cheshire Feline, and that's just the beginning. From exemplary writing to contemporary works, these catlike heroes and companions have caught the creative mind of perusers, becoming social images and adding to the rich embroidered artwork of abstract scenes.

1. **Prologue to Felines in Writing: A Murmur spective Outline**
1. **Felines as Abstract Images: Autonomy and Secret**

Felines, with their baffling characters, have filled in as representative figures in writing, addressing attributes like freedom, secret, and cunning. This segment gives an outline of the repetitive subjects related with felines in writing and makes way for a more profound investigation of explicit cat characters.

II. Old Scholarly Felines: Gatekeepers and Sidekicks

1. **Old Egyptian Felines: Watchmen of Life following death**
   In old Egyptian writing, felines assumed a huge part as defenders and mates. This segment dives into the imagery of felines in

antiquated Egyptian texts, investigating their relationship with gods, the hereafter, and the day to day routines of Egyptians.

2. Felines in Traditional Writing: Dreams and Allegories

Traditional writing, from crafted by Homer to the tales of Aesop, frequently highlighted felines as dreams and allegories. Whether as shrewd characters in tales or representative figures in awe-inspiring sonnets, felines left their paw prints on the pages of antiquated writing.

III. Middle age Felines in Writing: Old stories and Strange notions

1. Archaic Fables: Witches' Familiars and Signs

During the archaic period, felines became snared in old stories and odd notions. This part investigates the depiction of felines as familiars to witches, mystical creatures, and carriers of both great and awful signs in the writing of the time.

2. Chaucer's Murmur fect Journey: Felines in "The Canterbury Stories"

Geoffrey Chaucer, the dad of English writing, remembered felines for his perfect work of art, "The Canterbury Stories." This part dissects Chaucer's depiction of felines and their jobs in the accounts told by the travelers on their excursion.

IV. Renaissance Class: Felines in the Writing of Illumination

1. Shakespearean Hairs: Felines in the Poet's Plays

William Shakespeare, a scholarly monster of the Renaissance, integrated felines into his plays, injecting them with both emblematic and comedic importance. This segment investigates the different ways Shakespeare highlighted felines, from cunning wit to the jobs of cat characters in his works.

2. Felines as Figurative Figures: Renaissance Writing

In Renaissance writing, felines became figurative figures addressing honorability, secret, and freedom. This segment looks at how authors of the time used felines to convey more profound implications and subjects in their works.

V. Stubbles in Wonderland: The Cheshire Feline and Other Wonderland Cats

1. **Lewis Carroll's Capricious Felines: The Cheshire Feline and Then some**

   Lewis Carroll's "Alice's Undertakings in Wonderland" presented quite possibly of the most notable abstract feline — the Cheshire Feline. This part dives into the eccentric universe of Wonderland, investigating the imagery and philosophical insights encapsulated by the Cheshire Feline and other cat occupants.

2. **Felines in Hogwash Writing: Edward Lear and Then some**

Hogwash writing, with its energetic and ludicrous components, frequently included felines as unconventional characters. This segment looks at the commitments of creators like Edward Lear and their depiction of felines with regards to scholarly rubbish.

VI. Felines in Exemplary Writing: Rough looking Heroes and Companions

1. **The Feline in Exemplary Books: Dickens, Poe, and that's just the beginning**

   Exemplary books from the nineteenth century ahead frequently included felines as indispensable characters, going from Dickens' baffling cats to Poe's scary and representative dark feline. This part investigates how felines became scholarly friends and adversaries in exemplary writing.

2. **Felines in Fantasies: From Puss in Boots to Cinderella's Mice**

Fantasies, saturated with imagery and originals, much of the time included felines as mysterious and shrewd partners. This segment digs into the jobs of felines in exemplary fantasies, remembering the cleverness Puss for Boots and the groundbreaking cats in Cinderella.

VII. Felines in Kids' Writing: Cat Companions and Experiences

1. **Cherished Felines in Kids' Accounts: Winnie the Pooh, Beatrix Potter, and that's only the tip of the iceberg**
   Kids' writing has embraced felines as charming and courageous characters. This segment investigates the adored cat companions in works like A.A. Milne's Winnie the Pooh and Beatrix Potter's enchanting stories.
2. **Feline Secrets and Experiences: Enid Blyton and Then some**

Secret and experience stories for kids frequently include felines as analysts and partners. This part dives into the universe of feline secrets in kids' writing, analyzing crafted by Enid Blyton and different writers who rejuvenated cat characters.

VIII. Present day Scholarly Felines: From Smash hit Books to Realistic Books

1. **Artistic Felines in Top of the line Books: Murakami, Lord, and Gaiman**
   Contemporary writing, traversing kinds from mysterious authenticity to ghastliness, keeps on including felines as critical characters. This segment investigates the jobs of felines in top of the line books by writers like Haruki Murakami, Stephen Lord, and Neil Gaiman.
2. **Felines in Realistic Books: Cat Experiences in Consecutive Workmanship**

Realistic books have given a visual medium to depicting felines in writing. This segment dives into realistic books and comics that component felines as heroes, analyzing how craftsmen and authors rejuvenate cat undertakings through successive craftsmanship.

IX. Scholarly Felines in Mainstream society: Garfield, Felix, and Then some

1. **Garfield: The Languid, Lasagna-Adoring Abstract Feline**
   Jim Davis' Garfield, a lasagna-cherishing and ceaselessly languid feline, turned into a social symbol through comics and vivified transformations. This part examines the getting through ubiquity of Garfield and the effect of this famous cat character on writing and mainstream society.
2. **Felix the Feline: A Quiet Film Star and Then some**

Felix the Feline, perhaps of the earliest vivified character, rose above the quiet film time to turn into a darling symbol in movement. This part investigates the development of Felix and his persevering through heritage in writing and then some.

X. Web Felines: Artistic Impact in the Advanced Age

1. **Images, Viral Felines, and Abstract Motivations**
   In the computerized age, web felines have become social peculiarities. This part analyzes how artistic customs and originals impact the formation of web feline images, from Grouchy Feline to Nyan Feline.
2. **Abstract Felines in Online Entertainment: Instagram, Twitter, and Then some**

Web-based entertainment stages have become spaces for celebrating artistic felines. This part investigates the impact of exemplary and contemporary cat characters via online entertainment, where fans share their affection for abstract felines through hashtags, fan craftsmanship, and innovative substance.

XI.The Persevering through Tradition of Artistic Felines

1. **Cat Originals: From Antiquated Imagery to Present day Stories**

As we navigate the huge scene of writing, from old legends to contemporary blockbusters, the presence of felines as scholarly characters stays a steady. This end considers the persevering through tradition of cat prime examples, investigating how felines keep on enrapturing perusers' minds and add to the rich woven artwork of artistic practices.

2. **Felines in Writing and Then some: A Continuous Story**

The investigation of felines as scholarly characters is certainly not a static excursion yet a continuous story. This segment considers the eventual fate of cat characters in writing, guessing how felines will keep on molding stories, move writers, and charm perusers in the steadily developing universe of writing.

5.2Feline Inspirations in Visual Arts

Felines, with their polish, secret, and energetic disposition, have for some time been a wellspring of motivation for craftsmen across different mediums. From old figures to current computerized workmanship, cat themes have made a permanent imprint on the universe of visual expressions. This broad investigation dives into the rich history of felines in painting, figure, photography, and then some, analyzing how these perplexing animals have impacted and decorated the material of creative articulation.

1. **Presentation: The Appeal of Felines in Visual Expressions**
1. **The Getting through Allure of Cat Subjects**

Felines, with their enrapturing presence and different characters, have been repeating subjects in visual expressions from the beginning of time. This part presents the ageless charm of felines as dreams for craftsmen and gives an outline of the different imaginative developments and styles that have highlighted cat motivations.

II. Old Masterfulness: Cat Figures in Model and Artworks

1. **Egypt's Hallowed Felines: Figures and Works of art in the Nile Valley**
   In old Egypt, felines held a venerated status, representing eternality and security. This segment investigates the figures and canvases that embellished burial chambers, sanctuaries, and ordinary items, portraying felines as the two sidekicks and gatekeepers in the hereafter.

2. **Felines in Greek and Roman Workmanship: Baffling and Perky Themes**

In old Greek and Roman craftsmanship, felines took on multi-layered jobs, from secretive images to perky friends. This segment looks at the presence of felines in models, mosaics, and canvases, revealing insight into the developing creative translations of cat themes in traditional artifact.

III. Renaissance Class: Felines as Representations and Images

1. **Renaissance Specialists and Their Rough looking Subjects**
   During the Renaissance, specialists tracked down motivation in the style and beauty of felines. This part investigates the feline pictures of famous craftsmen, for example, Leonardo da Vinci and Albrecht Dürer, displaying how cat subjects became necessary to the visual language of the time.

2. **Imagery and Purposeful anecdote: Felines in Renaissance Craftsmanship**

As well as being depicted as individual subjects, felines filled in as emblematic figures in Renaissance craftsmanship. This segment digs into the metaphorical portrayals of felines, exemplifying characteristics like freedom, secret, and respectability, in progress of specialists like Titian and Giuseppe Arcimboldo.

IV. Authenticity and Impressionism: Catching Cat Substance

1. **Pragmatist Portrayals: Private Representations of Felines**
   Pragmatist specialists of the nineteenth century looked to catch the substance of their catlike subjects in itemized and sensible depictions. This segment investigates how craftsmen like Édouard Manet and Pierre-Auguste Renoir praised the magnificence and appeal of felines in their artistic creations.
2. **Impressionist Bristles: Felines in a Play of Light and Variety**

Impressionist painters, known for their imaginative utilization of light and variety, likewise directed their concentration toward felines. This segment analyzes how specialists like Pierre-Auguste Renoir and Édouard Manet mixed their catlike subjects with the lively energy and immediacy normal for the Impressionist development.

V. Oddity and Then some: Catlike Subjects in Cutting edge Craftsmanship

1. **Surrealist Felines: Caprice and Imagery in the Peculiar**
   Surrealist specialists, with their propensity for the strange and fantastical, frequently integrated felines into their vanguard works. This part investigates the strange and representative portrayals of felines in works of art by Salvador Dalí, René Magritte, and Max Ernst.
2. **Cat Subjects in Dynamic Expressionism and Pop Workmanship**

As craftsmanship developments advanced in the twentieth hundred years, felines kept on being noticeable subjects in different styles. This segment researches how felines showed up in progress of conceptual expressionist craftsmen like Jackson Pollock and in the pop workmanship manifestations of Andy Warhol, becoming symbols of contemporary visual culture.

VI. Felines in Contemporary Craftsmanship: From Authenticity to Extract Articulations

1. **Hyperrealism: Similar Feline Artworks and Figures**
   In contemporary workmanship, hyperrealism arose as a kind that tried to make similar portrayals of cat subjects. This segment investigates how specialists embraced hyperrealism to catch the mind boggling subtleties of felines, obscuring the lines among workmanship and reality.
2. **Felines in Road Craftsmanship and Paintings: Metropolitan Cat Motivations**

Road craftsmanship and paintings give an energetic material to cat motivations in contemporary metropolitan settings. This segment looks at how felines have become repeating subjects in road craftsmanship, adding to the vivid and dynamic visual scenes of urban communities all over the planet.

VII. Computerized Felines: Cat Subjects in the Time of Innovation

1. **Computerized Delineations and Feline Images: From Nyan Feline to Viral Workmanship**
   The computerized age delivered another material for cat motivations with the ascent of web felines and images. This part investigates how advanced artists and image makers transformed felines into notorious figures, with models, for example, Nyan Feline and Crotchety Feline becoming web sensations.
2. **Feline Craftsmanship in Expanded Reality and Virtual Spaces**

As innovation keeps on propelling, craftsmen investigate new boondocks in the domain of expanded reality (AR) and virtual spaces. This segment dives into how felines are coordinated into computerized workmanship encounters, offering watchers vivid experiences with cat subjects through AR and augmented reality (VR) stages.

VIII. Photography: Catching Cat Class and Liveliness

1. **Spearheading Feline Photographic artists: Félix Nadar and Harry Whittier Liberates**
   Photographic artists play had a urgent impact in catching the magnificence and appeal of felines from the perspective. This segment looks at the spearheading work of early feline photographic artists like Félix Nadar and Harry Whittier Liberates, who prepared for the catlike photography that followed.

2. **Web Felines At the center of attention: Naturally attractive Cat Superstars**

With the coming of the web, felines became photography stars, storing up worldwide followings through stages like Instagram. This segment investigates the peculiarity of web feline photography, including cat superstars like Lil Pal, Surly Feline, and Smoothie the Feline.

IX. Felines in Contemporary Figure: From Conventional to Vanguard

1. **Customary Feline Models: Bronze, Marble, and Earth**
   Customary figure strategies keep on being utilized to make ageless portrayals of felines. This part investigates how specialists use materials like bronze, marble, and dirt to create models that catch the substance of cat class and beauty.

2. **Cutting edge Feline Figures: Current Materials and Ideas**

In cutting edge mold, specialists explore different avenues regarding eccentric materials and ideas to push the limits of conventional portrayals. This segment analyzes how contemporary stone workers imbue advancement into their catlike manifestations, making figures that challenge discernments and welcome thought.

X. Felines in Establishment Craftsmanship and Mixed media Presentations

1. **Vivid Feline Establishments: Connecting with the Faculties**
   Establishment workmanship gives a stage to vivid encounters, and felines have become subjects and subjects in these tactile rich shows. This part investigates how craftsmen make establishments that draw in watchers in multisensory experiences with cat motivations.

2. **Mixed media Presentations: Felines in Advanced Craftsmanship Establishments**

Mixed media presentations combine innovation, sound, and visual craftsmanship to make dynamic and intuitive encounters. This segment examines how felines are coordinated into media craftsmanship establishments, where guests can draw in with cat topics through a mix of computerized projections, soundscapes, and material components.

XI. End: The Immortal Tradition of Cat Motivations in Visual Expressions

1. **Cat Style: From Antiquated Imagery to Present day Manifestations**
   As we explore the sweeping domain of visual expressions, from old models to contemporary computerized manifestations, the tradition of cat motivations stays a steady string. This end thinks about the persevering through tasteful allure of felines, analyzing how they keep on moving specialists across assorted mediums and styles.

2. **Felines in Visual Expressions and Society: Reflections and Social Effect**

Past their job as creative subjects, felines in visual expressions reflect more extensive social movements, cultural discernments, and the advancing connection among people and cats. This part considers the social effect of felines in visual expressions and their importance in forming visual stories from the beginning of time.

XII. Future Patterns and Prospects: Felines in Visual Expressions

1. **Mechanical Progressions: man-made intelligence Craftsmanship and Intuitive Displays**

   The fate of cat motivations in visual expressions is ready to embrace mechanical headways. This segment investigates arising patterns, for example, man-made intelligence produced craftsmanship and intelligent displays that influence innovation to make novel and connecting with encounters revolved around felines.

2. **Eco-Accommodating Craftsmanship Practices: Manageability in Cat Enlivened Manifestations**

As natural awareness develops, specialists are probably going to consolidate eco-accommodating practices into their cat propelled manifestations.

This part thinks about how maintainability and moral contemplations will impact the creation and utilization of feline themed craftsmanship later on.

5.3 The Cat in Cartoons and Comics

Felines, with their naughty shenanigans and charming appeal, have tracked down a unique spot in the realm of kid's shows and comics. This broad investigation digs into the rich history of cat characters in vivified kid's shows and successive craftsmanship, traversing from early paper comics to contemporary enlivened series. From notable characters like Tom and Jerry to the cherished Garfield, this excursion uncovers the development of felines as focal figures, companions, and comedic foils in the beautiful and creative domains of kid's shows and comics.

1. **Presentation: The Paws and Bristles of Activity and Comics**

1. Felines as Charming Characters: An Outline

Felines, with their particular characters and perky ways of behaving, have become dearest characters in the domain of kid's shows and comics. This segment presents the persevering through allure of cat characters and gives an outline of their development from the beginning of activity to the present.

II. Early Paper Comics: The Introduction of Cat Humor

1. The Katzenjammer Children and Other Spearheading Cat Appearances

In the mid twentieth hundred years, felines started showing up in paper comics. This part investigates the spearheading minutes when cat characters, frequently depicted in funny circumstances, became apparatuses in the realm of successive craftsmanship.

2. Krazy Kat: A Particular Cat Hero

George Herriman's "Krazy Kat" stands apart as an imaginative funny cartoon highlighting an idiosyncratic cat hero. This part looks at the strange and creative universe of Krazy Kat, investigating the effect of the strip on the depiction of felines in comics.

III. Brilliant Period of Liveliness: Cat Stars on the Cinema

1. Felix the Feline: The Principal Energized Cat Hotshot

In the beginning of liveliness, Felix the Feline arose as the principal vivified cat hotshot. This part digs into the historical backdrop of Felix, investigating his creation, notoriety, and persevering through heritage in the realm of vivified kid's shows.

2. Tom and Jerry: The Feline and-Mouse Dynamic

The feline and-mouse dynamic became the overwhelming focus with the presentation of Tom and Jerry. This segment breaks down the development of the notorious couple, investigating the comedic contention between the hapless feline Tom and the sharp mouse Jerry in a series that keeps on dazzling crowds around the world.

IV. The Ascent of Cat Hotshots: From Head honcho to Garfield

1. **Head honcho: The Head of the Stray Felines**
   "Head honcho," or T.C., arose as the head of a band of stray felines during the 1960s energized series. This segment investigates the appeal and mind of Big cheese, looking at how he turned into a social symbol and a portrayal of metropolitan cool in the realm of kid's shows.
2. **Garfield: The Apathetic, Lasagna-Cherishing Feline**

Jim Davis' creation, Garfield, turned into a social peculiarity in the late twentieth 100 years. This segment breaks down the qualities that make Garfield an immortal and engaging cat character, from his affection for lasagna to his laid-back demeanor.

V. Cat Charms in Vivified Elements: Disney and Then some

1. **The Aristocats: Disney's Exquisite Cat Gathering**
   Disney entered the universe of cat movement with "The Aristocats," highlighting a modern cast of cat characters. This segment investigates how Disney rejuvenated felines in enlivened highlights, underlining tastefulness, appeal, and musicality.
2. **Puss in Boots and Shrek: Cat Appeal in CGI Liveliness**

The coming of CGI activity welcomed additional opportunities for depicting felines on the big screen. This segment looks at the personality of Puss in Boots from the "Shrek" series, investigating how CGI innovation upgraded the visual allure and expressiveness of vivified cat characters.

VI. Cat Companions and Comedic Foils: Supporting Jobs in Kid's shows

1. **Sylvester and Tweety: The Quest for a Yellow Canary**
   Sylvester the Feline and Tweety Bird participated in an exemplary feline and-bird pursue in Looney Tunes and Merrie Songs kid's shows. This part investigates the comedic elements of Sylvester and Tweety, featuring the getting through ubiquity of their enlivened adventures.

2. **Stimpy and Ren: The Flighty Couple of Ren and Stimpy**

"Ren and Stimpy" presented a crazy and erratic cat character named Stimpy. This segment digs into the unpredictable and turbulent universe of Ren and Stimpy, investigating how the team tested customary animation standards with their contemptuous humor.

VII. Felines in Contemporary Energized Series: From Experience Time to Steven Universe

1. **Experience Time: The Mysterious Uneven Space Princess**
   "Experience Time" presented the mysterious Uneven Space Princess, a person with cat like elements and an extraordinary character. This segment investigates the innovative universe of "Experience Time" and the effect of Knotty Space Princess as a critical cat motivated character.

2. **Steven Universe and Lion: Mysterious Cat Mates**

"Steven Universe" highlighted an otherworldly and enchanted cat character named Lion. This part analyzes the meaning of Lion in the account, investigating how contemporary enlivened series consolidate cat components to improve narrating and character advancement.

VIII. Web Felines and Vivified Shorts: The Computerized Period of Cat Humor

1. **Simon's Feline: A Computerized Cat Sensation**
   The web time achieved another rush of cat humor with energized shorts like "Simon's Feline." This part investigates the outcome of

Simon Tofield's creation and its effect on the internet based scene of feline driven content.

2. **Feline Video Celebrations and Viral Liveliness**

Feline video celebrations turned into a social peculiarity, exhibiting the best of cat driven movement and recordings. This segment analyzes the ascent of feline video celebrations, investigating how they praise the appeal and humor of energized felines in the advanced age.

IX. Cat Motivations in Comics: From Garfield to Catwoman

1. **Garfield: The Lethargic Feline Who Vanquished the Comics Page**
Jim Davis' Garfield rose above vivified kid's shows to turn into a staple of paper comics. This segment investigates the getting through ubiquity of Garfield in the realm of successive craftsmanship, breaking down how the lasagna-adoring feline vanquished the comics page.

2. **Catwoman: Cat Femme Fatale in Comic Book Legend**

In the domain of comic books, Catwoman arose as a complicated and notorious person. This part digs into the historical backdrop of Catwoman, investigating her development from a feline thief to a complex and getting through figure in the DC Comic books universe.

X. Autonomous Comics and Realistic Books: Cat Stories Past Standard

1. **Blacksad: Noir Stories with Human Cats**
"Blacksad" is a noir comic series highlighting human characters, with the protagonist being a feline investigator. This segment looks at how free comics and realistic books investigate cat accounts past standard shows, consolidating rich narrating with special visual styles.

2. **The Rabbi's Feline: Unusual Stories of a Talking Cat**

"The Rabbi's Feline" is a realistic novel that mixes humor and other-worldliness, highlighting a talking feline. This segment investigates how realistic books like "The Rabbi's Feline" utilize cat characters to tell unusual stories and address further subjects.

XI. Social Effect and Imagery: The Feline as Model in Kid's shows and Comics

1. **Felines as Original Figures: Autonomy, Secret, and Eccentricity**

   Cat characters in kid's shows and comics frequently epitomize original characteristics, addressing autonomy, secret, and caprice. This part dives into the social effect and imagery of felines as model figures in the domains of activity and consecutive workmanship.

2. **Felines as Impressions of Human Way of behaving and Society**

Past their comedic and fantastical components, cat characters in kid's shows and comics act as impressions of human way of behaving and cultural elements. This part investigates how felines are utilized as illustrations and mirrors for investigating human encounters, connections, and social peculiarities.

XII. Future Patterns and Prospects: Felines in Activity and Comics

1. **Variety in Cat Portrayal: Comprehensive Stories in Liveliness**

   The eventual fate of cat characters in liveliness is probably going to see expanded variety and portrayal. This part investigates how makers are integrating different points of view and accounts into energized stories, giving a more comprehensive depiction of cat characters.

2. **Intelligent and Vivid Feline Comics: The Development of Consecutive Craftsmanship**

With progressions in innovation, intuitive and vivid encounters might shape the eventual fate of feline driven comics. This segment looks at arising patterns in intelligent narrating and how they might impact the development of consecutive craftsmanship revolved around cat characters.

Chapter 6

Cats in Music And Entertainment

Felines, with their confounding charm and lively characters, have made a permanent imprint on the universe of music and diversion. This broad investigation digs into the rich embroidery of cat motivations, looking at their presence in melodies, films, TV programs, theater creations, and then some. From ageless melodic organizations commending felines to notable cat characters in films, this excursion disentangles the agreeable connection among felines and the assorted domains of music and amusement.

1. **Presentation: The Catlike Tune in Diversion**
1. **Felines as Dream and Similitude: An Outline**

Felines, with their effortlessness and persona, have been a lasting dream for craftsmen in the domain of music and diversion. This part presents the persevering through allure of cat motivations, investigating their representative importance and social effect in different types of amusement.

II. Felines in Traditional Music: From Stravinsky to the Stray Feline Swagger

1. **Stravinsky's "Feline's Support" and Melodic Eccentricity**
   Traditional writers have drawn motivation from felines, imbuing their organizations with cat eccentricity. This segment investigates Igor Stravinsky's "Feline's Support" and other old style pieces that catch the substance of felines through complex melodic plans.
2. **Rossini's "Duetto buffo di due gatti" and Operatic Energy**

Gioachino Rossini's "Duetto buffo di due gatti," or the Feline Two part harmony, is an unusual operatic piece that energetically impersonates the hints of felines. This segment dives into the appeal of Rossini's structure and its persevering through fame as an entertaining melodic tribute to cat shenanigans.

III. Jazz and Blues: The Murmur fect Notes of Cat Impact

1. **Howl Blend: Jazz Felines and the Language of Spontaneous creation**
   Jazz, with its improvisational nature, has invited the impact of felines into its melodic language. This part investigates how jazz performers have integrated cat propelled themes and extemporization into their sytheses, making a dynamic and expressive melodic discourse.
2. **Soul-filled Felines and Catfish Blues: Cat Subjects in Blues Music**

The blues, known for its deep articulations, has likewise embraced cat subjects. This segment inspects how blues performers have woven the persona and liveliness of felines into their verses and tunes, from "Dark Feline Bone" to "Catfish Blues."

IV. Felines on Broadway: Dramatic Stubbles and Melodic Stories

1. **Felines: The Murmur fect Melodic Party**
   Andrew Lloyd Webber's "Felines" remains as a milestone in cat enlivened dramatic creations. This part dives into the universe of "Felines," investigating its beginnings, influence, and getting through ubiquity as a historic melodic that brings T.S. Eliot's verse to life on the Broadway stage.

2. **Aristocats and Then some: Catlike Stories in Melodic Theater**

Past "Felines," different creations have investigated cat stories on the Broadway stage. This segment inspects how musicals like Disney's "The Aristocats" variation and unique creations with cat characters have added to the different scene of melodic theater.

V. Film Scores and Soundtracks: Cat Harmonies on the Big Screen

1. **Disney's The Lion Ruler: Cat Magnificence in Film Scores**
   Film scores and soundtracks assume a pivotal part in upgrading the realistic experience, and felines have frequently been highlighted unmistakably in these sytheses. This part investigates the glorious cat harmonies in Disney's "The Lion Lord" and other film scores that praise the majesty and persona of felines on the big screen.

2. **Puss in Boots and Shrek: Cat Furrows in Energized Soundtracks**

Energized films have presented paramount cat characters with similarly charming soundtracks. This part analyzes the melodic scores of "Puss in Boots" from the "Shrek" series and other vivified soundtracks that enhance the appeal of energized felines through music.

VI. Feline Tunes in Famous Music: From Lost Feline Swagger to The Lovecats

1. **Lost Feline Swagger: The Swing of the Homeless Felines**
   The Lost Felines burst onto the music scene with their rockabilly hit "Homeless Feline Swagger." This segment investigates how the tune turned into a hymn for cat propelled strut and what it meant for the rockabilly type.
2. **The Lovecats and Other Feline Tastic Hits**

The Fix's "The Lovecats" and other feline tastic hits have become famous in well known music. This segment dives into how performers across classes have made significant feline melodies, from capricious tunes to ardent anthems praising the exceptional connection among people and cats.

VII. Cat Subjects in Music Recordings: Picturing Feline Roused Songs

1. **Feline Recordings and Melodic Peculiarities on the Web**
   With the ascent of the web, feline recordings and melodic peculiarities have become interwoven. This segment investigates the social effect of feline themed music recordings, from viral sensations to coordinated efforts among artists and cat forces to be reckoned with.
2. **Essential Feline Appearances in Music Recordings**

Artists frequently integrate cat companions into their music recordings, adding an additional layer of appeal to the visual narrating. This part features important feline appearances in music recordings, exhibiting how felines improve the account and style of these creations.

VIII. Felines in TV: Energized Series, Ads, and that's only the tip of the iceberg

1. **The Simpsons and the Feline Woman: Energized Cat Farces**
   "The Simpsons" has highlighted significant cat minutes, including the scandalous Feline Woman character. This segment

investigates how energized series utilize cat spoofs and characters to imbue humor and parody into their storylines.

2. Felines in Ads: Promoting with Cat Appeal

TV ads frequently influence the appeal of felines to catch crowd consideration. This part analyzes how felines have become notorious figures in promoting, from feline food advertisements to noteworthy cat spokes-felines.

IX. Felines in Gaming: Melodic Scores and Intuitive Cat Undertakings

1. **Neko Atsume and the Murmur fect Gaming Soundtrack**
Gaming encounters highlighting felines frequently incorporate spellbinding melodic scores. This part investigates the melodic appeal of games like "Neko Atsume," where players cooperate with virtual felines in a capricious and loosening up climate.

2. **Cat Topics in Computer game Soundtracks**

Computer games including felines consolidate different melodic styles to improve the gaming experience. This segment dives into the catlike subjects found in computer game soundtracks, displaying how music adds to the vivid universe of intelligent feline undertakings.

X. Feline VIPs in Diversion: From Cantankerous Feline to Lil Pal

1. **Grouchy Feline: The Image Sensation Turned Melodic Star**
Web feline superstars have risen above the advanced domain to become stars in different types of amusement. This part investigates the melodic undertakings of Surly Feline and other cat powerhouses who have wandered into the universe of music and diversion.

2. **Lil Buddy and the Mysterious Sound of Room Feline**

Lil Buddy, known for her particular appearance, likewise wandered into the domain of music with the arrival of "Science and Sorcery: A Soundtrack to the Universe." This segment looks at how Lil Pal's melodic venture adds an unusual aspect to the universe of cat propelled diversion.

XI. Cat Motivations in Webcasts and Sound Creations

1. **Feline Topic Web recordings: Murmuring Stories and Cat Undertakings**
   Web recordings committed to felines have arisen as an exceptional type of cat enlivened diversion. This segment investigates feline themed webcasts, highlighting murmuring stories, interviews with feline specialists, and conversations on the universe of cat friendship.
2. **Feline ASMR and Loosening up Cat Soundscapes**

ASMR (Independent Tactile Meridian Reaction) channels committed to felines give audience members loosening up cat soundscapes. This segment dives into the relieving universe of feline ASMR and how it has turned into a famous decision for those looking for quieting hearable encounters.

XII. Social Effect and Imagery: The Feline as Performer and Dream

1. **Felines as Social Symbols: Amusement Past Species**
   Cat characters and forces to be reckoned with have become social symbols, rising above their species. This segment investigates the social effect of felines as performers and dreams, thinking about how they catch the creative mind of crowds around the world.
2. **Felines as Motivations for Inventive Articulation**

Past their jobs as performers, felines motivate imaginative articulation in different structures. This segment digs into the imagery of felines in music and diversion, looking at how their presence enhances creative stories and associates with crowds on a significant level.

XIII. Future Patterns and Prospects: Felines in Developing Diversion Scenes

1. **Virtual Shows and computer based intelligence Created Cat Exhibitions**
   The eventual fate of cat motivated amusement might include virtual shows and simulated intelligence produced exhibitions. This segment investigates arising patterns in virtual diversion and how innovation is reshaping the manners by which felines are highlighted in melodic and visual encounters.

2. **Intelligent Diversion Encounters: Computer generated Reality and Then some**

As innovation propels, intuitive diversion encounters including felines might become the dominant focal point. This segment looks at the capability of augmented reality and other intelligent stages in making vivid and participatory cat roused diversion.

XIV. The Persevering through Tune of Felines in Music and Amusement

1. **Cat Concordance: A Reflection on Melodic Heritages**
   All in all, the persevering through tune of felines in music and diversion is a demonstration of the immortal and widespread allure of these cryptic animals. This part considers the rich embroidery of cat propelled amusement, commending the agreeable connection among felines and the different domains of imaginative articulation.

2. **The Continuous Story: Felines as Everlasting Performers**

The story of felines in music and amusement is progressing, with each murmur, yowl, and hair adding to the never-ending appeal of these everlasting performers. This last segment mulls over the future parts in the cat propelled story, expecting the proceeded with reverberation of felines in the always developing scenes of music and diversion.

6.1 Musicians and Their Feline Companions

Cats have been charming the existences of performers for a really long time, filling in as steadfast friends, motivations, and even dreams. This broad investigation dives into the agreeable connections between prestigious artists and their cherished cat companions. From traditional arrangers to shake legends, jazz virtuosos to pop sensations, this excursion reveals the significant and frequently capricious associations among performers and the catlike mates who share their lives.

1. **Presentation: Paws, Hairs, and Crescendos**
1. **The Connection Among Performers and Felines: An Outline**

The connection among performers and felines is an ensemble of friendship, motivation, and common getting it. This segment presents the significant associations between prestigious artists and their catlike mates, making way for an investigation of these novel and frequently eccentric bonds.

II. Felines in Traditional Music: Creating with Cat Effortlessness

1. **Mozart and His Cherished Murmur tner, Large Kitty**
   Wolfgang Amadeus Mozart, perhaps of the best old style writer, imparted his life to a darling cat friend named Enormous Kitty. This part dives into the archived records of Mozart's friendship for felines and the potential impact Enormous Kitty might have had on the maestro's inventive approach.
2. **Beethoven's Warmth for Cats: The Writer and His Mousie**

Ludwig van Beethoven, known for his strong and emotive pieces, was likewise a feline darling. This segment investigates Beethoven's affection for his feline, Mousie, and the accounts that uncover the delicate minutes between the arranger and his catlike companion.

III. Jazz Felines: Extemporizations and Stubble Jerking Rhythms

1. **John Coltrane's Catlike Motivations: The Affection for His Felines**

   John Coltrane, a jazz saxophonist and writer, tracked down comfort and motivation within the sight of his felines. This segment investigates Coltrane's affection for his catlike buddies and how their quieting impact might have molded the climate of his melodic practices and exhibitions.

2. **Billie Occasion's Feline Songs: The Woman and Her Catlike Companions**

Billie Occasion, the famous jazz vocalist, had a profound association with felines all through her life. This segment dives into the catlike serenades that went with Occasion's unbelievable voice, looking at the effect of felines on her own and creative excursion.

IV. Rock Legends and Their Catlike Team: From Freddie Mercury to David Bowie

1. **Freddie Mercury's Felines: The Imperial Friends of a Stone Symbol**

   Freddie Mercury, the charming frontman of Sovereign, imparted his home to a large number of felines. This part investigates the grand presence of Mercury's catlike sidekicks and the extraordinary connection between the stone legend and his adored felines.

2. **David Bowie's Feline from Japan: A Catlike Companion Named Mickey**

David Bowie, the visionary stone and pop symbol, had a unique cat companion named Mickey. This segment reveals the narrative of

Bowie's feline and the job Mickey played in the existence of the artist known for his consistently advancing persona and imagination.

V. Murmur sonalities in Popular Music: Taylor Quick and Ed Sheeran

1. **Taylor Quick's Catlike Crew: Meredith, Olivia, and Benjamin**
   Taylor Quick, the worldwide pop sensation, is known for her profound friendship for felines. This segment investigates the characters of Quick's catlike crew — Meredith, Olivia, and Benjamin — and the brief looks at their lively associations that Quick offers with her fans.

2. **Ed Sheeran's Fuzzy Dream: Graham the Little cat**

Ed Sheeran, the vocalist lyricist with a deep voice, found motivation in a shaggy companion named Graham. This part digs into Sheeran's association with Graham and the effect the lively little cat had on the artist's life and innovative approach.

VI. Feline Mates in Down home Music: Johnny Money and Cart Parton

1. **Johnny Money's Warmth for Felines: The Man dressed in Dark and His Shaggy Companions**
   Johnny Money, the unbelievable "Man dressed in Dark," had a weakness for felines all through his profession. This part investigates Money's friendship for cat buddies and the accounts that uncover the delicate minutes between the nation symbol and his felines.

2. **Cart Parton's Affection for Felines: Rough looking Companions in the Nation Spotlight**

Cart Parton, the cherished blue grass music symbol, shares her existence with a few felines. This segment dives into Parton's affection for her unshaven companions, investigating how her catlike buddies give pleasure and friendship to the acclaimed vocalist and lyricist.

VII. Felines in the Musical Metal Scene: Nightwish and Their Catlike Charms

1. **Tuomas Holopainen's Feline Driven Structure: Music for Cats**
   Tuomas Holopainen, the genius behind the musical metal band Nightwish, formed a collection enlivened by felines. This segment investigates Holopainen's feline driven arrangement, "Music for Little cats," and the capricious combination of metal and cat subjects.

2. **Nightwish's Catlike Mascot: Tarja the Feline**

Nightwish, known for their pretentious and dramatic sound, has a catlike mascot named Tarja. This segment digs into the band's association with felines, looking at the job of Tarja as a representative and fun loving presence in the realm of musical metal.

VIII. Cat Companions in Hip-Jump: Sneak Homeboy and Run the Gems

1. **Sneak Homeboy's Catlike Colleagues: Felines and Hip-Bounce Eminence**
   Sneak Homeboy, a hip-jump symbol, has a weakness for felines and frequently shares his affection for cat sidekicks via web-based entertainment. This part investigates the charming minutes between Sneak Homeboy and his felines, exhibiting the hip-jump craftsman's fondness for his fuzzy companions.

2. **Run the Gems and Their Feline Collection: Howl the Gems**

Run the Gems, the powerful hip-jump pair, left on a special task named "Whimper the Gems," where their music was remixed with feline sounds. This part investigates the imaginative and perky undertaking that combined hip-bounce and cat impacts in a startling coordinated effort.

IX. Old style Felines in the Cutting edge Time: 2Cellos and Their Unshaven Companion

1. **2Cellos and Pitz the Feline: Traditional Instruments and Cat Liveliness**
   2Cellos, the powerful cello pair, presented a catlike sidekick named Pitz into their universe of old style music. This segment investigates the energetic collaborations among 2Cellos and Pitz, exhibiting how traditional performers track down delight and motivation within the sight of their catlike companions.
2. **Web Sensation: 2Cellos' Exhibitions with Felines**

2Cellos turned into a web sensation with their exhibitions high-lighting felines. This segment dives into the viral outcome of 2Cellos' recordings, where their old style music blends with the fanciful notion of felines, catching the hearts of crowds all over the planet.

X. The Unshaven Side of Elective Music: PJ Harvey and Kurt Cobain

1. **PJ Harvey's Catlike Artist: Felines and Elective Inventiveness**
   PJ Harvey, the powerful elective stone performer, has imparted her life to cat friends. This segment investigates the wonderful association between PJ Harvey and her felines, considering how cat presence entwines with the innovative soul of elective music.
2. **Kurt Cobain's Felines: Cat Companions of the Grit Symbol**

Kurt Cobain, the notable frontman of Nirvana, had a profound fondness for felines. This segment dives into Cobain's relationship with his catlike companions and the brief looks at family life that gave equilibrium to the turbulent universe of grit music.

XI. Felines and Non mainstream People: Iron and Wine and Armada Foxes

1. **Iron and Wine's Catlike Cover Workmanship: Felines in Non mainstream People Style**

   Iron and Wine, the non mainstream people project drove by Sam Bar, highlighted cat enlivened cover workmanship for one of their collections. This part investigates the crossing point of felines and non mainstream society style, analyzing how cat symbolism improves the visual personality of artists in the independent scene.

2. **Armada Foxes' Feline Appearance: Non mainstream People Harmonies and Bristly Companions**

Armada Foxes, known for their ethereal non mainstream society harmonies, remembered a feline appearance for one of their music recordings. This part digs into the unconventional coordinated effort between Armada Foxes and a catlike companion, adding a hint of appeal to the band's visual narrating.

XII. Felines in Underground Rock: Squint 182 and the Troublemaker Cat Mentality

1. **Squint 182's Catlike Collection Cover: Felines in Underground Rock Defiance**

   Squint 182, the notable underground rock band, embraced cat symbolism with a collection cover highlighting a feline. This part investigates the troublemaker cat mentality of Flicker 182, looking at how felines turned into an image of defiance and perkiness in the realm of underground rock.

2. **Punk Felines and Do-It-Yourself Soul: Cats in the Troublemaker Scene**

Felines have become famous figures in the troublemaker scene, exemplifying the Do-It-Yourself soul and defiant ethos of the class. This part digs into the presence of felines in underground rock culture, from collection covers to cat colleagues going with punk artists on visit.

XIII. The Tradition of Performers and Their Catlike Partners: A Coda

1. **Cat Inheritances: Felines and the Persevering through Effect on Melodic Imagination**

   All in all, the tradition of performers and their catlike partners is a demonstration of the persevering through connection among people and felines. This segment thinks about the significant effect of felines on melodic inventiveness, commending the delight, motivation, and friendship that catlike companions bring to the existences of performers.

2. **The Continuous Ensemble: Felines and Future Crescendos in Music**

The story of performers and their catlike partners is progressing, with each murmur, howl, and melodic note adding to the continuous ensemble of cat propelled inventiveness. This last segment thinks about the future parts in the amicable account among artists and their rough looking dreams, expecting the proceeded with reverberation of felines in the steadily advancing universe of music.

6.2 Theatrical Cats: Broadway's "Cats" Phenomenon

Broadway has seen incalculable creations that have made a permanent imprint on the universe of theater, yet few have accomplished the unbelievable status of "Felines." This thorough investigation dives into the cryptic peculiarity that is "Felines," looking at its starting points, influence, social importance, and the getting through appeal of cat sorcery that has enthralled crowds around the world.

1. **Presentation: Lurking into Broadway's Feline Tastrophe**
1. **The Fascinating Reason: Felines on the Jellicle Ball**

"Felines," with its eccentric reason of felines gathering for the Jellicle Ball, quickly caught the creative mind of theatergoers. This segment presents the remarkable universe of "Felines," making way for a profound jump into its creation, development, and social effect.

II. The Creation of "Felines": From T.S. Eliot to Andrew Lloyd Webber

1. **T.S. Eliot's "Old Possum's Book of Reasonable Felines" as Source Material**

   The excursion of "Felines" starts with T.S. Eliot's assortment of sonnets, "Old Possum's Book of Viable Felines." This part investigates how Andrew Lloyd Webber found and adjusted Eliot's capricious stanzas into a pivotal melodic, preparing for the introduction of "Felines."

2. **Andrew Lloyd Webber's Melodic Authority: Making the Jellicle Soundtrack**

Andrew Lloyd Webber, the melodic virtuoso behind "Felines," made an entrancing soundtrack that turned into a vital piece of the creation's prosperity. This part dives into Lloyd Webber's innovative approach, the piece of notorious melodies, and the melodic components that characterized the Jellicle experience.

III. The Ascent of the Jellicle Clan: Broadway Introduction and Worldwide Achievement

1. **Broadway Debut: The Jellicle Ball Becomes the overwhelming focus**

   "Felines" made its Broadway debut in 1982 at the Colder time of year Nursery Theater, denoting the start of a dramatic peculiarity. This segment investigates the underlying gathering, basic recognition, and the one of a kind dramatic encounter that the Jellicle Clan brought to the stage.

2. **Worldwide Visiting and Global Achievement: Murmur fecting the Jellicle Wizardry**

Following its prosperity on Broadway, "Felines" left on a worldwide excursion, enamoring crowds on global stages. This part inspects the social effect and gathering of "Felines" as it howled its direction into the hearts of theater lovers all over the planet.

IV. The Jellicle Experience: Dramatic Components and Ensemble Plan

1. **Inventive Set Plan: Rejuvenating the Junkyard**
   The set plan of "Felines" is a visual display, changing the stage into an enchanted junkyard where the Jellicle Felines show some major signs of life. This segment dives into the imaginative set plan that submerged crowds in the unusual universe of cat dream.
2. **Elaborate Ensemble Plan: The Catsuit Annals**

Ensemble fashioner John Napier assumed a crucial part in rejuvenating the Jellicle Felines with his unpredictable and creative plans. This segment investigates the advancement of ensemble plan in "Felines," featuring the difficulties and developments that added to the particular cat tasteful.

V. The Dance of the Jellicles: Movement and Development

1. **Gillian Lynne's Murmur fect Movement: The Dance of the Jellicles**
   Choreographer Gillian Lynne assumed a pivotal part in molding the rawness and development of the Jellicle Felines. This segment investigates Lynne's choreographic commitments, the mark dance styles of the Jellicles, and the effect of development in conveying the catlike substance in front of an audience.
2. **Jellicle Ball: The Dance Scene that Charmed Crowds**

The Jellicle Ball, a focal component in the melodic, is a dance scene that exhibits the different characters of the Jellicle Felines. This segment analyzes the movement and meaning of the Jellicle Ball, featuring its part in character improvement and narrating.

VI. Famous Characters of the Jellicle Clan: From Grizabella to Mr. Mistoffelees

1. **Grizabella the Excitement Feline: Dramatic Reclamation and Profound Reverberation**

   Grizabella, the Fabulousness Feline, is a focal person whose excursion pulls at the heartstrings of crowds. This segment digs into the personality of Grizabella, her close to home curve, and the effect of her notable tune, "Memory," which became inseparable from the melodic.

2. **Mr. Mistoffelees and Other Jellicles: The Unique Cast of Characters**

The Jellicle Clan brags a different cast characters, each with its own one of a kind character and commitment to the story. This segment investigates the powerful characters of "Felines," from the otherworldly Mr. Mistoffelees to the wicked Rum Tum Tugger, disentangling the layers of cat intricacy.

VII. Basic Praise and Grants: The Murmur fection of "Felines"

1. **Broadway Honors: Tony Grants and Record-Breaking Accomplishments**

   "Felines" got far and wide basic approval and various awards during its Broadway run. This part features the renowned Tony Grants won by the creation and the record-breaking accomplishments that cemented its spot in the chronicles of theater history.

2. **Worldwide Effect: Rising above Language and Culture**

Past its prosperity on Broadway, "Felines" made a permanent imprint worldwide, rising above language and social boundaries. This part looks at the global acknowledgment and effect of "Felines," setting its status as a dramatic peculiarity with a general allure.

VIII. Recoveries and Reimaginings: The Continuous Tradition of "Felines"

1. **Broadway Restorations: Getting back to the Jellicle Ball**
   "Felines" encountered a few Broadway restorations, each carrying a new viewpoint to the Jellicle story. This part investigates the restorations of "Felines," looking at how chiefs and imaginative groups moved toward the reconsidering of this notorious melodic for new ages of crowds.

2. **Film Variation: Felines on the Big Screen**

In 2019, "Felines" took its jump from the stage to the cinema with a ritzy film transformation. This segment digs into the difficulties and debates encompassing the film, investigating the realistic translation of the Jellicle Ball and the gathering it earned.

IX. The Social Effect of "Felines": Images, Farces, and Tributes

1. **Images and Farces: Catnip for Web Culture**
   "Felines" turned into a peculiarity in web culture, motivating endless images, spoofs, and hilarious transformations. This segment investigates the viral presence of "Felines" in web-based spaces and its startling effect on computerized imagination and humor.

2. **Praises and Accolades: The Getting through Heritage in Mainstream society**

The tradition of "Felines" reaches out past the stage and screen, impacting different features of mainstream society. This part looks at the reverences and accolades paid to "Felines" in TV, music, and different types of amusement, exhibiting its persevering through engrave on the social scene.

X. Debates and Reactions: Investigating the Jellicle Excursion

1. **Creative Decisions and Debates: A Troublesome Gathering**
   While "Felines" delighted in monstrous achievement, it likewise confronted its portion of debates and reactions. This segment investigates the troublesome gathering of specific imaginative decisions, from the utilization of computerized fur innovation in the film transformation to more extensive evaluates of the melodic's account and subjects.

2. **Social Awareness and Advancing Points of view**

As cultural points of view advance, so too do conversations around social awareness in imaginative portrayals. This part looks at how "Felines" has been reconsidered with regards to evolving sensibilities, tending to worries and cultivating discussions about inclusivity and portrayal.

XI. The Jellicle Heritage: Reflections on "Felines" in the 21st Hundred years

1. **Immortal Allure: The Never-ending Appeal of the Jellicles**
   In spite of the discussions and studies, "Felines" keeps an immortal appeal that keeps on resounding with crowds. This segment considers the persevering through allure of the Jellicle Felines, investigating why the melodic has held its supernatural charm as the decades progressed.

2. **Dramatic Impact: Felines in the Embroidered artwork of Broadway History**

As a dramatic peculiarity, "Felines" has unquestionably transformed the embroidery of Broadway history. This segment mulls over the impact of "Felines" on the development of melodic theater, analyzing its commitments to the artistic expression and its enduring effect on ensuing ages of theater makers.

XII. Future Possibilities and the Jellicle Continuum

1. **Heritage in the 21st 100 years: Adjusting the Jellicle Story**
   The tradition of "Felines" endures into the 21st hundred years, with progressing conversations about its place in contemporary theater. This part investigates the possible transformations, restorations, and reevaluations that might shape the fate of the Jellicle continuum.

2. **The Jellicle Ball Lives On: Expecting the Following Demonstration**

As the Jellicle Felines keep on lurking across stages and screens, the expectation for the following demonstration of their otherworldly excursion stays substantial. This last area considers the continuous tradition of "Felines" and the possibility of the Jellicle Ball charming new crowds in the years to come.

6.3 Cats in Film and Television

Felines, with their baffling appeal and fun loving characters, have for quite some time been a wellspring of motivation for narrators in the domains of film and TV. This broad investigation dives into the complex jobs that felines play in artistic and televisual accounts. From famous feline characters to significant feline exhibitions, this excursion unwinds the different manners by which cats have transformed the cinema and the little screen, enhancing narrating and enthralling crowds around the world.

1. **Presentation: The Catlike Focal point on the Silver and Little Screens**
1. **Felines as True to life and Televisual Symbols: An Outline**

The presence of felines in film and TV traverses classifications and periods, from quiet movies to contemporary blockbusters and gorge commendable series. This segment presents the overall topics of cat impact in visual narrating, making way for a far reaching investigation of felines in the realm of moving pictures.

II. Felines in Quiet Film: Spearheading Cat Presence on Screen

1. **The Appearance of Film Felines: Early Quiet Film Period**
Felines made their presence felt in the beginning of film, with quiet movies highlighting cat entertainers in jobs that went from comedic to strange. This part investigates the spearheading long periods of film felines, looking at their jobs and importance in the quiet time.

2. **Félix the Feline: Activity's Most memorable Cat Whiz**

Félix the Feline, a formation of illustrator Pat Sullivan, became perhaps the earliest vivified genius in the quiet film time. This part digs into the starting points of Félix, his effect on movement, and the getting through tradition of this unusual cat character.

III. The Brilliant Period of Hollywood: Felines as On-Screen Sidekicks

1. **Hollywood Charm and Cat Mates: Felines in Exemplary Movies**
The Brilliant Time of Hollywood carried with it a variety of exemplary movies highlighting paramount cat friends. This part investigates how felines were incorporated into exemplary Hollywood stories, filling in as images of polish, secret, and friendship.

2. **The Feline Appearance Peculiarity: Hitchcock, Monroe, and Then some**

Alfred Hitchcock's propensity for remembering felines for his movies turned into a striking peculiarity, and notorious figures like Marilyn

Monroe embraced cat friendship on and off-screen. This segment digs into the feline appearance pattern, analyzing its pervasiveness in Hollywood during the mid-twentieth hundred years.

IV. Movement Renaissance: Felines in Disney and Then some

1. **Disney's Aristocats: Energized Cat Style**
   Disney's "The Aristocats" remains as a milestone in vivified films highlighting cat heroes. This segment investigates the formation of the film, the characters that populate its beguiling account, and the effect of "The Aristocats" in the liveliness renaissance time.

2. **Tom and Jerry: Feline and-Mouse Hijinks in Liveliness**

The exemplary enlivened couple of Tom and Jerry, with Tom being the feline bad guy, turned into a staple of energized diversion. This part digs into the persevering through allure of Tom and Jerry, investigating their feline and-mouse hijinks and the development of their characters throughout the long term.

V. Felines as Symbols of Frightfulness: From Dark Felines to Outsider Xenomorphs

1. **Odd notion and Imagery: Felines With sickening apprehension Film**
   Felines have frequently been related with odd notion and imagery, and this has converted into their jobs with dismay films. This part investigates the depiction of felines with dismay film, from dark felines as signs to cat enlivened heavenly elements.

2. **Outsider Felines: Cat Propelled Extraterrestrial Detestations**

The idea of outsider felines takes a remarkable turn in the domain of sci-fi repulsiveness. This segment analyzes what cat motivation has meant for the production of extraterrestrial animals, from the xenomorphs in the "Outsider" establishment to supernatural feline like creatures.

VI. Cat Film Stars: Genuine and Vivified Exhibitions

1. Genuine Felines as Celebrities: The Catlike Entertainers of Hollywood

Genuine felines have graced the cinema as gifted entertainers by their own doing. This segment investigates the tales of genuine cat entertainers, from the quiet film period to contemporary film, and the difficulties and delights of working with these shaggy actors.

2. Enlivened Feline Exhibitions: Voice Acting and Portrayal

Enlivened felines, rejuvenated through voice acting and activity, have become notable characters in their own respect. This part looks at the specialty of voice representing enlivened felines, investigating how entertainers rejuvenate cat characters through their exhibitions.

VII. The Ascent of Feline Narratives: Genuine Stories and Protection

1. Feline Narratives: Investigating the Universe Of all shapes and sizes Felines

Narratives have given a stage to investigate the existences of both homegrown and wild felines. This part digs into the ascent of feline narratives, from inspiring accounts of homegrown felines to preservation shone stories that shed light on the situation of huge felines.

2. Enormous Feline Narratives: Preservation and Mindfulness

Narratives zeroing in on enormous felines add to preservation endeavors and bring issues to light about the difficulties these grand animals face. This segment investigates how producers and traditionalists utilize the medium to advocate for the insurance of large feline species around the world.

VIII. Felines in TV Series: From Vivified Comedies to Dramatizations

1. **Vivified Feline Comedies: The Simpsons, Big cheese, and that's just the beginning**
   Vivified TV series have embraced the comedic capability of cat characters. This part investigates enlivened feline comedies, from the misfortunes of Snowball II in "The Simpsons" to the tricks of Head honcho and his posse.

2. **Sensational Cat Presence: Felines in television Shows and Secrets**

Felines assume huge parts in TV shows and secrets, frequently filling in as sidekicks or baffling components in plotlines. This part inspects how felines are coordinated into the accounts of TV series, adding layers of feeling, interest, and imagery.

IX. Cat Impacts in Dream and Science fiction TV

1. **Supernatural Felines: Dream Series with Charming Cat Characters**
   Dream TV series frequently include mysterious felines with supernatural capacities. This part investigates the presence of mystical felines in dream series, from vivified shows like "Sabrina: The Enlivened Series" to true to life top picks like "Enchanted."

2. **Science fiction Felines: Extraterrestrial and Advanced Cat Elements**

In the domain of sci-fi TV, felines take on extraterrestrial and advanced jobs. This segment looks at how felines are depicted in science fiction series, from outsider cat creatures to advanced automated felines that cross the universe.

X. Feline Driven Comedies: Garfield, Doraemon, and Then some

1. **Garfield: The Languid Feline with an Affection for Lasagna**
   Garfield, the lasagna-adoring and Mondays-abhorring feline, turned into a notable person in the realm of funny cartoons and energized TV. This segment investigates the social effect of Garfield, from the comics to vivified transformations.

2. **Doraemon: Japan's Mechanical Feline from What's in store**

Doraemon, a mechanical feline from what's to come, has turned into a dearest character in Japanese mainstream society. This part digs into the persevering through prevalence of Doraemon, looking at how the advanced cat has caught the hearts of crowds around the world.

XI. Web Felines: From Viral Sensations to Web Series

1. **Viral Feline Recordings: Web Sensations and Worldwide Distinction**
   The web has impelled felines to worldwide fame through viral recordings. This segment investigates the peculiarity of viral feline recordings, from Console Feline to Cranky Feline, and their effect on web culture.

2. **Web Series Featuring Felines: Simon's Feline and Nyan Feline Experiences**

Web series have embraced felines as focal characters, making engaging and charming substance for online crowds. This part analyzes well known web series featuring felines, including "Simon's Feline" and the experiences of the web renowned Nyan Feline.

XII. Felines As a general rule TV: Cat Stars and Contests

1. **Cat Stars Truly television: Ability Shows and Pet Rivalries**
   Unscripted tv has displayed the abilities and characters of genuine felines in rivalries and grandstands. This part investigates how felines become stars in all actuality television, from ability contests to pet-focused series that celebrate cat beguile.

2. Feline Unscripted TV dramas: Investigating Cat Conduct and Connections

Unscripted TV dramas revolved around felines give bits of knowledge into cat conduct and connections. This segment looks at feline driven unscripted TV dramas, for example, "My Feline from Damnation" and "Jackson System's Absolute Feline Magic," and their part in teaching watchers about cat care and conduct.

XIII. Felines in Film and TV Promoting: From Mascots to Stars

1. Cat Mascots: Felines in Marking and Promoting

Felines have become famous mascots for brands, adding a bit of appeal and appeal to publicizing efforts. This part investigates the utilization of felines as mascots in marking, from the modern appeal of the Cheshire Feline to the lively shenanigans of the Yowl Blend felines.

2. Felines in Business Movies: From Whiskas to Catvertising Patterns

Business films highlighting felines have turned into a well known pattern, with brands profiting by the boundless allure of cat stars. This segment looks at catvertising patterns, investigating how felines become the overwhelming focus in plugs for pet items, family products, and then some.

XIV. The Social Effect of Felines in Film and TV

1. Cat Models: Imagery and Social Importance

Felines, with their different characters and imagery, have made a permanent imprint on culture. This part investigates cat prime examples in film and TV, analyzing how felines are frequently used to convey explicit characteristics, from secret and freedom to friendship and enchantment.

2. Felines as Web-based Entertainment Forces to be reckoned with: The Force of Paws in the Advanced Age

The ascent of web-based entertainment has transformed felines into compelling figures with gigantic web-based followings. This part investigates the peculiarity of felines as web-based entertainment forces to be reckoned with, looking at how stages like Instagram have raised cat stars to big name status.

XV. Discussions and Reactions: Examining Cat Portrayals

1. Creature Government assistance Concerns: Moral Contemplations in Cat Exhibitions
As attention to creature government assistance develops, so do worries about the treatment of felines in film and TV. This part analyzes moral contemplations in cat exhibitions, addressing discussions and reactions connected with the utilization of felines in media outlets.

2. Generalizations and Deceptions: Cat Sayings in Media

Generalizations and deceptions of felines in media can propagate destructive sayings. This segment investigates normal cat figures of speech in film and TV, addressing how certain depictions might add to confusions about felines and their way of behaving.

XVI. Future Patterns and Prospects: Felines in Developing Visual Narrating

1. Headways in Movement and CGI: The Fate of Cat Characters
As innovation advances, so do the opportunities for making practical and fantastical cat characters through liveliness and CGI. This segment investigates the eventual fate of cat characters in film and TV, taking into account how progressions in innovation might shape their depictions.

2. Comprehensive Narrating: Addressing Assorted Cat Encounters

The eventual fate of felines in film and TV includes more comprehensive narrating, addressing the different encounters of cat characters. This part inspects the potential for narrating that embraces various varieties, ways of behaving, and connections, encouraging a more extravagant and more exact portrayal of felines.

7

Chapter 7

Cat Cafés And Pop Culture Phenomena

In the steadily advancing scene of mainstream society, one peculiarity has caught the hearts and minds of feline darlings around the world - the Feline Bistro. This investigation leaves on a brilliant excursion into the beginnings, worldwide spread, and social effect of Feline Bistros, unwinding the appeal of these foundations where caffeine meets feline friendship. From the primary murmurs of the idea to the flourishing pattern it has become, we dig into the purposes for their notoriety, the extraordinary encounters they offer, and the more extensive ramifications of Feline Bistros as a huge social and social peculiarity.

1. **Presentation: Preparing Caffeine and Cat Delight**
1. **The Feline Bistro Idea: Where Espresso Meets Feline Friendship**

The idea of Feline Bistros mixes the mitigating appeal of espresso culture with the fun loving and soothing presence of felines. This part presents the peculiarity, investigating the underlying flashes of motivation that prompted the production of these remarkable foundations.

II. The Introduction of Feline Bistros: From Taiwan to the World

1. **Taiwan's Feline Blossom Nursery: The Trailblazer**
   The excursion of Feline Bistros started in Taipei, Taiwan, with the kickoff of Feline Bloom Nursery in 1998. This segment dives into the spearheading endeavors of Feline Bloom Nursery, investigating how it prepared for the worldwide Feline Bistro frenzy.
2. **Japan's Neko no Jikan: Feline Bistros Go Standard**

Japan assumed a crucial part in promoting Feline Bistros, with Neko no Jikan (Feline's Time) opening in Osaka in 2004. This part investigates how Japan embraced the idea and shot it into the standard.

III. The Worldwide Murmur spread: Feline Bistros All over the Planet

1. **Catfé Parlor in North America: Carrying Cat Rapture toward the West**
   The Feline Bistro pattern didn't take long to jump across mainlands. This segment investigates the presentation of Feline Bistros in North America, zeroing in on pioneers like Catfé Parlor in Vancouver, Canada.
2. **Europe's Catlike Asylums: Feline Bistros Across the Landmass**
   Europe immediately embraced the Feline Bistro pattern, with foundations springing up in significant urban communities. This part investigates the spread of Feline Bistros across Europe, featuring key areas and their special commitments to the pattern.
3. **Asia's Relationship with Feline Bistros: Past Japan and Taiwan**

While Japan and Taiwan launched the Feline Bistro peculiarity in Asia, different nations on the landmass embraced the pattern with energy. This segment investigates how Feline Bistros turned into a social peculiarity in nations like South Korea and Thailand.

IV. The Catfé Experience: Caffeine, Felines, and Local area

1. **The Catfé Equation: Espresso, Felines, and Association**
   Feline Bistros offer a novel mix of espresso culture and cat friendship. This part investigates the Catfé experience, from the cautiously arranged espresso menus to the comfortable spaces intended for human and cat cooperation.

2. **The Reverberation of Unwinding: Stress Alleviation and Treatment**
   Feline Bistros are commended for their helpful advantages, giving supporters a break from the burdens of day to day existence. This part digs into the mental and profound parts of investing energy in Feline Bistros, investigating how the quieting presence of felines adds to pressure alleviation.

3. **Associating with Felines and People: Encouraging Associations**

Feline Bistros give a social space where feline sweethearts can interface with similar people. This segment investigates the social elements of Feline Bistros, from solo visits for unwinding to bunch trips and even occasions that advance local area commitment.

V. The Catlike Stars: Felines as Bistro Envoys

1. **Feline Choice and Government assistance: Focusing on Cat Prosperity**
   The prosperity of the inhabitant felines is a main concern for Feline Bistros. This part investigates how Feline Bistros select and really focus on their catlike diplomats, guaranteeing that the climate is advancing and peaceful for the inhabitant felines.

2. **Cat Characters: The Appeal of Bistro Felines**

Each feline has an extraordinary character, and Feline Bistros commend the uniqueness of their catlike occupants. This part presents some eminent bistro felines, featuring their beguiling qualities and the jobs they play in making an inviting climate.

VI. Catfé Culture and Product: From Mugs to Whimper chandise

1. **Feline themed Style and Product: Bringing the Bistro Home**
   Feline Bistros frequently expand their exceptional appeal past the actual space. This segment investigates the feline themed style and product presented by Feline Bistros, from mugs decorated with paw prints to yowl chandise that permits benefactors to take a piece of the bistro experience home.
2. **Catfé Occasions and Studios: Cat Fun Past Espresso**

To improve the Catfé experience, numerous foundations have occasions and studios revolved around felines. This part investigates the assorted scope of exercises presented by Feline Bistros, from yoga meetings with felines to instructive studios on cat care.

VII. Difficulties and Discussions: Exploring the Catfé Scene

1. **Wellbeing and Cleanliness Concerns: Adjusting Feline Government assistance and Client Security**
   The mix of felines and food foundations raises wellbeing and cleanliness concerns. This segment investigates the difficulties Feline Bistros face in keeping a perfect and safe climate for the two felines and supporters.
2. **Social Awareness: Exploring Alternate points of view on Feline Government assistance**

Feline government assistance guidelines shift internationally, and Feline Bistros should explore social contrasts and assumptions. This part digs into the social awareness expected in laying out and working Feline Bistros, addressing discussions and reactions connected with cat government assistance.

VIII. Feline Bistros in Mainstream society: From Network programs to Catfé Merchandise

1. **Feline Bistros in Media: TV Highlights and Mainstream society References**
Feline Bistros have advanced into well known media, becoming highlighted attractions on TV programs and moving references in mainstream society. This segment investigates how Feline Bistros are depicted and celebrated in different types of media.
2. **Catfé Product and Coordinated efforts: Broadening the Brand**

The progress of Feline Bistros has prompted the formation of feline themed product and coordinated efforts. This segment investigates how Feline Bistros influence their image, cooperating with specialists and organizations to make novel items that allure for feline sweethearts.

IX. Catfé The travel industry: The Ascent of Cat Journeys

1. **Catfé The travel industry Patterns: Going for Cat Rapture**
Feline Bistros have become objections for feline cherishing voyagers, igniting a pattern known as Catfé the travel industry. This part investigates the ascent of Catfé the travel industry, from fans visiting well known Feline Bistros to coordinated feline themed travel encounters.
2. **Social Trade and Global Catfé Organizations**

Catfé the travel industry cultivates social trade and the formation of worldwide organizations among Feline Bistros. This part investigates how Feline Bistros work together across borders, sharing bits of knowledge and making a worldwide local area of cat cherishing foundations.

X. Future Patterns and the Catfé Development

1. **Catfé Developments: Virtual Encounters and Then some**
As Feline Bistros keep on advancing, inventive ideas are forming

the fate of the Catfé experience. This part investigates arising patterns, from virtual Feline Bistros to innovation improved cooperations, guessing how the idea might adjust to evolving times.

2. Feline Bistros Past Espresso: Enhancing the Experience

The Catfé peculiarity is growing past customary espresso driven models. This part investigates how Feline Bistros are broadening their contributions, integrating components like themed occasions, feline driven libraries, and coordinated efforts with nearby organizations.

XI. The Charming Tradition of Feline Bistros

1. Catfé Sorcery: A Murmur sonal Inheritance

All in all, the Feline Bistro peculiarity has woven an extraordinary embroidery of cat charm, espresso culture, and local area. This last segment thinks about the getting through tradition of Feline Bistros, commending their commitment to mainstream society, cat government assistance promotion, and the making of spaces where felines and people can share snapshots of happiness, unwinding, and association.

2. The Continuous Pawsibility: Expecting the Following Part in Catfé History

As Feline Bistros proceed to flourish and catch the minds of feline darlings universally, the expectation for the following part in Catfé history is unmistakable. This closing section examines the continuous pawsibility of Feline Bistros, imagining the job they might play in molding future patterns in the realm of cat propelled mainstream society.

7.1 The Emergence of Cat Cafés Worldwide

Over the most recent twenty years, a beguiling and imaginative idea has surprised the world - the Feline Bistro. Starting in Taipei, Taiwan, and quickly spreading across Asia, Europe, North America, and then some, Feline Bistros have become something beyond spots to taste espresso; they are remarkable asylums where benefactors can enjoy the delight of cat friendship. This extensive investigation unfurls the story of Feline Bistros around the world, following their unassuming starting points, analyzing their fast worldwide expansion, and disentangling the social effect of these captivating foundations.

1. **Presentation: The Unshaven Blend - Beginnings of Feline Bistros**
1. **The Beginning in Taiwan: Feline Blossom Nursery**
The account of Feline Bistros begins with the kickoff of Feline Bloom Nursery in Taipei, Taiwan, in 1998. This part digs into the motivation and conditions that prompted the foundation of the world's most memorable Feline Bistro, presenting the idea that would enthrall the hearts of feline darlings universally.
2. **Catfé Culture: Blending Caffeine and Friendship**

The primary thought behind Feline Bistros rotates around consolidating the delights of espresso culture with the relieving presence of felines. This part presents the center idea of Feline Bistros, underlining the novel mix of caffeine and cat friendship that characterizes these foundations.

II. Feline Bistros in Asia: Trailblazers and Murmur ogress

1. **Japan's Neko no Jikan: An Impetus for Worldwide Catfé Frenzy**
Japan assumed a vital part in promoting Feline Bistros on a worldwide scale. The launch of Neko no Jikan in Osaka in 2004 denoted a huge defining moment. This segment investigates Japan's commitment to the Catfé frenzy and the social factors that filled its prosperity.
2. **Asia's Catlike Asylums: Past Taiwan and Japan**

The Feline Bistro pattern quickly extended past Taiwan and Japan, penetrating the texture of other Asian nations. This segment investigates the expansion of Feline Bistros in South Korea, Thailand, China, and different countries, featuring the assorted social settings that embraced these foundations.

III. The Catfé Transformation in Europe: Embracing Cat Appeal

1. **Feline Bistros in Europe: A Mainland Cat Undertaking**
   Feline Bistros tracked down a warm welcome in Europe, with foundations springing up in significant urban communities. This segment follows the spread of Feline Bistros across the mainland, investigating key areas, social subtleties, and the particular appeal that European Feline Bistros bring to the worldwide stage.

2. **North America's Catfé Culture: A Cross-Mainland Jump**

The Catfé peculiarity advanced across the Atlantic to North America, where it kept on thriving. This segment looks at the presentation of Feline Bistros in North America, zeroing in on pioneers like Catfé Parlor in Vancouver and the ensuing development of Catfé culture in the district.

IV. The Catfé Experience: Blending Caffeine, Cat Happiness, and Local area

1. **The Catfé Equation: Creating a Murmur fect Experience**
   Feline Bistros are more than spots to partake in some espresso; they offer a special encounter where benefactors can loosen up in the organization of cat companions. This part investigates the components that comprise the Catfé equation, from the espresso menu to the cautiously arranged feline climate.

2. **Catfé Culture: Unwinding, Treatment, and Mingling**

The Catfé experience stretches out past espresso and felines, including unwinding, remedial advantages, and amazing open doors for mingling. This part digs into the diverse parts of Catfé culture, analyzing how supporters track down comfort, happiness, and association in these catlike shelters.

V. The Catlike Stars: Feline Diplomats and Their Characters

1. **Organizing Feline Stars: Choice and Government assistance**
Feline Bistros cautiously select their catlike occupants, guaranteeing their prosperity is a main concern. This segment investigates the most common way of organizing feline stars, from the standards for choosing inhabitant felines to the actions taken to establish an agreeable and improving climate for them.

2. **The Appeal of Bistro Felines: Characters and Jobs**

Each feline in a Feline Bistro has an extraordinary character, adding to the general appeal of the foundation. This part presents some outstanding bistro felines, investigating their singular characteristics and the jobs they play in making an inviting and engaging climate.

VI. Catfé Culture Past Espresso: Product, Occasions, and that's only the tip of the iceberg

1. **Feline themed Product: Expanding the Bistro Experience**
Feline Bistros frequently broaden their image through feline themed stock. This part investigates the universe of Catfé stock, from mugs and shirts to yowl chandise that benefactors can bring back home, permitting them to drag out the Catfé experience.

2. **Catfé Occasions and Studios: Cat Fun Past Espresso**

To improve the Catfé experience, numerous foundations have occasions and studios revolved around felines. This part investigates the assorted scope of exercises presented by Feline Bistros, from yoga meetings with felines to instructive studios on cat care.

VII. Catfé Difficulties and Debates: Exploring the Catlike Scene

1. **Adjusting Feline Government assistance and Client Wellbeing: Wellbeing and Cleanliness**
   The mix of felines and food foundations raises wellbeing and cleanliness concerns. This segment investigates the difficulties Feline Bistros face in keeping a spotless and safe climate for the two felines and supporters, tending to wellbeing guidelines, and best practices.

2. **Social Awareness: Exploring Alternate points of view**

Feline government assistance principles shift all around the world, and Feline Bistros should explore social contrasts and assumptions. This part digs into the social responsiveness expected in laying out and working Feline Bistros, addressing debates and reactions connected with cat government assistance.

VIII. Feline Bistros in Mainstream society: From television Elements to Catfé Merchandise

1. **Feline Bistros in Media: TV Elements and Mainstream society**
   Feline Bistros have become highlighted attractions on network shows and motivated references in mainstream society. This segment investigates how Feline Bistros are depicted and celebrated in different types of media, from narratives and travel shows to fictitious portrayals.

2. **Catfé Product and Joint efforts: Broadening the Brand**

The progress of Feline Bistros has prompted the production of feline themed product and joint efforts. This segment investigates how Feline Bistros influence their image, collaborating with craftsmen and organizations to make one of a kind items that enticement for feline sweethearts.

IX. Catfé The travel industry: Cat Journeys and Global Organizations

1. **Catfé The travel industry Patterns: Going for Cat Euphoria**
   Feline Bistros have become objections for feline cherishing explorers, igniting a pattern known as Catfé the travel industry. This segment investigates the ascent of Catfé the travel industry, from devotees visiting popular Feline Bistros to coordinated feline themed travel encounters.
2. **Social Trade and Global Catfé Organizations**

Catfé the travel industry cultivates social trade and the production of global organizations among Feline Bistros. This part investigates how Feline Bistros team up across borders, sharing experiences and making a worldwide local area of cat cherishing foundations.

X. Future Patterns and the Catfé Development

1. **Catfé Advancements: Virtual Encounters and Then some**
   As Feline Bistros keep on developing, imaginative ideas are forming the fate of the Catfé experience. This segment investigates arising patterns, from virtual Feline Bistros to innovation improved connections, guessing how the idea might adjust to evolving times.
2. **Feline Bistros Past Espresso: Expanding the Experience**

The Catfé peculiarity is growing past conventional espresso driven models. This segment investigates how Feline Bistros are differentiating their contributions, consolidating components like themed occasions, feline driven libraries, and joint efforts with neighborhood organizations.

7.2 Cat Festivals and Events

As of late, the world has seen a murmur fect peculiarity that joins feline sweethearts, lovers, and cat colleagues in glad festival - Feline Celebrations and Occasions. These social events, going from capricious celebrations to instructive meetings, have turned into a vital piece of worldwide cat culture. This broad investigation divulges the dynamic woven artwork of Feline Celebrations and Occasions, digging into their starting points, various structures, social importance, and the significant effect they have on the common appreciation for our catlike companions.

1. **Presentation: The Ascent of Feline Celebrations**
1. **Cat Holidays Released: The Development of Feline Celebrations**
   The idea of Feline Celebrations and Occasions has picked up speed, advancing into lively festivals that unite feline sweethearts and lovers.
   This part presents the general subject of Feline Celebrations, investigating their ascent in prevalence and the common love for everything cat.
2. **The Social Meaning of Feline Celebrations**

Feline Celebrations have risen above simple social affairs; they convey social importance, mirroring the profound connection among people and felines. This segment dives into the social parts of Feline Celebrations, looking at how these occasions add to the worldwide festival of felines in different social orders.

II. The Spearheading Feline Celebrations: A Verifiable Point of view

1. **The Early Years: Starting points of Feline Celebrations**
   The underlying foundations of Feline Celebrations can be followed back to explicit occasions and drives that laid the basis for the broad festival of felines. This segment investigates the early long periods of Feline Celebrations, featuring key minutes and powerhouses that formed their development.
2. **CatCon: The Impetus for Present day Feline Festivals**

CatCon, established in 2014, remains as a crucial occasion that ignited the cutting edge period of Feline Celebrations. This part analyzes the origin of CatCon, its advancement throughout the long term, and the job it played in forming the scene of feline driven social affairs.

III. Sorts of Feline Celebrations and Occasions

1. **Unusual Feline Celebrations: Observing Cat Bliss**
   Some Feline Celebrations center around the unusual and energetic parts of feline culture, offering a space for giggling, diversion, and euphoria. This segment investigates unusual Feline Celebrations, from feline themed marches to outfit challenges, and their job in making a carefree air.

2. **Instructive Feline Meetings: Cultivating Information and Mindfulness**

Instructive Feline Meetings act as stages for feline specialists, veterinarians, and devotees to share information and examine significant issues connected with cat government assistance. This segment analyzes the meaning of instructive Feline Meetings, featuring key occasions and their effect on feline support.

IV. Worldwide Feline Celebrations: A Visit All over the Planet

1. **The Nekonomics of Japan: Feline Culture in the Place that is known for the Rising Sun**
   Japan has a rich history of praising felines, and this part investigates how Feline Celebrations in Japan, like the Neko no Hello (Feline Day), feature the country's profound social association with cats.

2. **Catvidfest: A Virtual Cat Festivity**
   In the age of the web, Catvidfest arose as a virtual festival of feline recordings. This segment dives into the computerized domain of Catvidfest, investigating how online stages have turned into a novel stage for cat merriments.

3. **The UK's Catfest: A Combination of Workmanship, Music, and Cat Reverence**

   Catfest in the Unified Realm is a diverse occasion that joins craftsmanship, music, and a profound love for felines. This part investigates the extraordinary components of Catfest and its commitment to the social embroidered artwork of feline festivals.

4. **The Feline Fair in Argentina: A South American Cat Spectacle**

South America has embraced the Feline Festival in Argentina as an energetic festival of cat culture. This part investigates the Feline Fair and its effect on encouraging a feeling of local area among feline sweethearts in the district.

V. Local area and Association: The Social Elements of Feline Celebrations

1. **Cat Companionships: Building People group at Feline Celebrations**

   Feline Celebrations act as stages for feline devotees to interface, share encounters, and construct enduring fellowships. This part investigates the social elements of Feline Celebrations, looking at how these occasions cultivate a feeling of local area among participants.

2. **Feline Bistro Joint efforts: Spanning Bistros and Celebrations**

Feline Bistros frequently team up with Feline Celebrations, making cooperative energies that improve the general insight for participants. This segment dives into the cooperative endeavors between Feline Bistros and Celebrations, investigating how these associations add to the outcome of both.

VI. VIP Felines and Forces to be reckoned with: Murmuring into the Spotlight

1. **The Ascent of VIP Felines: From Cranky Feline to Lil Buddy**
Big name felines have become notorious figures, enrapturing the hearts of millions all over the planet. This segment investigates the peculiarity of VIP felines, their effect on Feline Celebrations, and how their presence adds a bit of star capacity to these occasions.

2. **Virtual Entertainment Forces to be reckoned with: Felines Overwhelming the Advanced Domain**

The computerized age has led to cat web-based entertainment powerhouses, with felines gathering enormous followings on stages like Instagram and TikTok. This segment looks at the impact of virtual entertainment felines and how their attendance is utilized at Feline Celebrations.

VII. The Matter of Feline Celebrations: Brands, Product, and Sponsorships

1. **Feline Celebrations as Undertakings: Financial Effect**
As Feline Celebrations fill in fame, they additionally become worthwhile undertakings. This part investigates the financial effect of Feline Celebrations, analyzing how they create income through ticket deals, sponsorships, and product.

2. **Feline themed Product: Broadening the Celebration Experience**

Feline Celebrations frequently include a plenty of feline themed stock, from clothing to embellishments. This segment investigates the universe of Feline Celebration stock, featuring how these things add to the general celebration experience.

VIII. Difficulties and Reactions: Exploring Issues in Feline Celebration Culture

1. **Moral Contemplations: Feline Government assistance and Celebration Practices**
The festival of felines at celebrations raises moral contemplations, especially concerning the government assistance of cat members. This part digs into the difficulties and reactions encompassing Feline Celebrations, resolving issues connected with feline government assistance and dependable occasion rehearses.

2. **Inclusivity and Variety: Cultivating an Inviting Climate**

Feline Celebrations mean to be comprehensive spaces for all feline darlings, paying little mind to foundation or character. This part investigates the significance of inclusivity and variety in Feline Celebration culture, tending to difficulties and offering bits of knowledge into establishing inviting conditions.

IX. Future Patterns and Advancements in Feline Celebrations

1. **Mixture Models: Mixing Physical and Virtual Encounters**
As innovation progresses, Feline Celebrations are investigating mixture models that mix physical and virtual encounters. This segment investigates arising patterns, from virtual feline shows to expanded reality components, forming the fate of Feline Celebrations.

2. **Worldwide Joint effort: The Potential for Global Feline Celebrations**

The worldwide allure of Feline Celebrations opens the entryway for global coordinated effort. This segment investigates the potential for worldwide associations and the making of uber occasions that join feline darlings from around the world.

7.3 CatCon: The Ultimate Celebration of Cat Culture
In the domain of cat merriments, CatCon remains as a signal, drawing feline lovers, superstar felines, and industry specialists into a novel festival of everything feline. Since its beginning in 2014, CatCon

has developed from a basic plan to a worldwide peculiarity, making a space where the adoration for felines rises above limits. This investigation dives into the beginnings, advancement, importance, and effect of CatCon, looking at how it has turned into a definitive festival of feline culture.

1. **Presentation**
1. **The Introduction of CatCon: From Idea to The real world**
   CatCon arose as the brainchild of Susan Michals, a carefully prepared columnist and feline fan. This part investigates the underlying idea driving CatCon, its pioneer's obsession for felines, and the vision that pushed the making of this earth shattering occasion.
2. **CatCon's Debut Year: Setting the Stage**

The debut CatCon in 2014 established the groundwork for what might turn into a yearly festival of cat culture. This segment considers the features of CatCon's most memorable year, analyzing the key components that set up for its future achievement.

II. CatCon: Something other than a Show

1. **Past the Conventional: CatCon's One of a kind Methodology**
   CatCon separates itself from traditional shows by mixing diversion, instruction, and a profound love for felines. This segment investigates how CatCon's extraordinary methodology catches the embodiment of feline culture, making it a unique occasion in the catlike world.
2. **The Superstar Feline Element: Drawing Cat Stars and Fans**

A significant draw of CatCon is the presence of big name felines that have acquired distinction via web-based entertainment. This part investigates how the incorporation of these catlike stars adds a dash of charm to CatCon, drawing fans from around the world.

III. CatCon As the years progressed

1. **Development of CatCon: From Unassuming Starting points to Worldwide Sensation**
   CatCon has gone through huge development and change since its origin. This segment follows the development of CatCon as the years progressed, investigating how it has extended in extension, participation, and impact.

2. **Important Minutes: Features from CatCon's Set of experiences**

Throughout the long term, CatCon has seen important minutes that lastingly affect participants and the worldwide feline adoring local area. This part returns to probably the most eminent features, from big name appearances to historic declarations.

IV. The CatCon Experience

1. **The CatCon Commercial center: A Famous hub for Feline Sweethearts**
   The CatCon Commercial center is a focal center where participants can investigate a huge swath of feline related items, administrations, and developments. This segment digs into the commercial center, featuring the different contributions that make it a central hub for feline darlings.

2. **Boards, Studios, and Courses: Supporting Cat Information**
   CatCon goes past diversion, offering a stage for schooling through boards, studios, and courses. This part investigates how these meetings add to the improvement of participants' information about feline consideration, conduct, and prosperity.

3. **Craftsmanship and Inventiveness: CatCon as a Material for Cat Articulation**

Craftsmen and makers track down an interesting space at CatCon to exhibit their cat enlivened works. This part investigates the imaginative side of CatCon, from feline themed works of art and figures to special and imaginative manifestations that celebrate felines in different structures.

V. Big name Felines and Powerhouses at CatCon

1. Web Big names: CatCon's Top notch Visitors

One of the characterizing highlights of CatCon is the presence of web renowned felines and their proprietors. This part features probably the most adored cat famous people that have graced CatCon, enthralling the hearts of fans with their appeal and uniqueness.

2. Superstar Feline Meet-and-Welcomes: A Murmur sonal Experience

CatCon gives an uncommon chance to fans to meet their number one web feline VIPs face to face. This segment investigates the meet-and-welcome meetings, inspecting the fervor and happiness these associations bring to participants.

VI. The Effect of CatCon on Feline Culture

1. CatCon's Effect on Cat Patterns

CatCon plays had a critical impact in forming cat drifts and impacting how felines are seen in mainstream society. This part investigates how CatCon has added to the ascent of feline culture and the expanded perceivability of felines in traditional press.

2. Encouraging People group: CatCon as an Impetus for Associations

Past the celebrations, CatCon fills in as an impetus for building a worldwide local area of feline fans. This segment looks at how CatCon encourages associations among participants, making a feeling of kinship that reaches out past the actual occasion.

VII. Difficulties and Reactions

1. **Adjusting Business Interests and Feline Government assistance**

    As CatCon keeps on developing, it faces difficulties in offsetting business interests with the prosperity of the felines in question. This part investigates the moral contemplations and reactions encompassing CatCon, addressing concerns connected with feline government assistance and dependable occasion rehearses.

2. **Expanding Inclusivity: Tending to Portrayal and Availability**

CatCon, similar to any enormous scope occasion, faces difficulties connected with inclusivity and availability. This part digs into endeavors made by CatCon to address these difficulties, advancing variety and guaranteeing the occasion is open to a wide crowd.

VIII. The Fate of CatCon

1. **Advancements and Developments: CatCon's Continuous Advancement**

    CatCon keeps on advancing, presenting new developments and growing its span. This segment investigates what's in store patterns and potential extensions that might shape the continuous development of CatCon.

2. **Worldwide Impact: CatCon's Effect on Global Feline Culture**

CatCon's impact reaches out past the lines of the US, motivating feline related occasions and get-togethers internationally. This part inspects how CatCon has turned into a guide for global feline culture, impacting comparable occasions all over the planet.

IX. CatCon's Persevering through Heritage

1. **CatCon as a Social Peculiarity**

   All in all, CatCon has risen above its status as a show to turn into a social peculiarity that commends the greatness of felines. This last segment ponders CatCon's getting through heritage, its effect on feline culture, and the job it plays in encouraging a worldwide appreciation for our catlike buddies.

2. **Expecting the Following Section: CatCon's Continuous Murmur spective**

As CatCon keeps on captivating feline darlings around the world, the expectation for the following section in its set of experiences stays substantial. This finishing up portion examines CatCon's continuous murmur spective, imagining what's in store patterns and developments that will shape a definitive festival of feline culture.

Chapter 8

Cats As Symbols Of Social Movements

Felines, with their baffling charm and mysterious way of behaving, have procured a spot in our homes as well as arisen as strong images inside the domain of social developments. From old human advancements to the cutting edge period, felines play played different parts, developing from venerated figures to famous portrayals of opposition, autonomy, and social change. This investigation plans to dig into the complex account of felines as images of social developments, analyzing their verifiable importance, social effect, and the exceptional job they play in passing on messages of dispute, fortitude, and transformation.

B. The Omnipresence of Felines: From Antiquated Egypt to Web Images

Felines have a rich and fluctuated history, highlighting conspicuously in the legends and imagery of various societies. This segment sets the stage by following the verifiable universality of felines, investigating their adored status in antiquated civic establishments like Egypt and their contemporary resurgence as web big names and images.

II. Antiquated Imagery of Felines

1. **Felines in Antiquated Egypt: Gatekeepers and Heavenly Colleagues**
   In old Egypt, felines held a sacrosanct and venerated status, related with divinities like Bastet. This segment digs into the imagery of felines in antiquated Egyptian culture, analyzing their jobs as defenders, images of ripeness, and heavenly sidekicks.

2. **Felines in Antiquated Rome and Greece: Blended Imagery**

While antiquated Rome saw felines with doubt, partner them with strange notions and black magic, old Greece portrayed them as images of opportunity and autonomy. This part investigates the blended imagery of felines in traditional artifact.

III. Archaic Europe: Felines and Strange notions

1. **Felines and Black magic: The Dull Periods of Cat Oppression**
   Middle age Europe saw a change in discernment as felines, especially dark felines, became related with odd notions and black magic.
   This part investigates the dull periods of cat mistreatment, inspecting how felines were many times substitutes during witch chases.

2. **Felines as Familiars: Fantasy and Reality**

The faith in felines as familiars, heavenly sidekicks of witches, added layers of intricacy to cat imagery during the middle age time frame. This segment digs into the fantasies and real factors encompassing felines as familiars.

IV. Renaissance and Edification: Felines in Workmanship and Writing

1. **Felines in Renaissance Craftsmanship: Images of Polish and Secret**
   The Renaissance saw a resurgence of interest in felines, depicting

them as images of tastefulness and secret in workmanship. This segment investigates the portrayal of felines in compositions and writing during this period.

2. **Illumination Period: Felines and Realism**

The Illumination got a shift perspectives towards creatures, and felines started to be viewed as animals deserving of logical request and perception. This part analyzes what the Illumination time meant for the view of felines and their consideration in logical talk.

V. Felines in Political Kid's shows and Parody

1. **Political Parody and Felines: Paws in Legislative issues**
   Political kid's shows have a long history of utilizing creatures, including felines, as emblematic portrayals of political figures and belief systems. This part investigates the utilization of felines in political parody and their job in passing on complex political messages.

2. **Felines as Political Figures: Purposeful anecdotes and Cartoons**

Over the entire course of time, felines have been represented as political figures in humorous outlines. This segment digs into the symbolic portrayals of felines as political pioneers, investigating the subtleties of these personifications.

VI. Felines in Current Social Developments

1. **Web Feline Images: The Introduction of a Social Peculiarity**
   The web upset how felines are seen in mainstream society. This segment investigates the introduction of web feline images, following their development from early discussions to the far reaching peculiarity they are today.

2. **Testy Feline and Viral Contradiction**

Testy Feline, with her interminably disappointed articulation, accidentally turned into a symbol of dispute and opposition. This segment digs into the surprising ascent of Testy Feline and her effect on the crossing point of felines and virtual entertainment activism.

VII. Felines in Civil rights Developments

1. **Felines and Woman's rights: Strengthening and Freedom**
   Felines have shown up in women's activist developments, representing autonomy, versatility, and strengthening. This part investigates the presence of felines in women's activist iconography and their job in passing on messages of orientation balance.

2. **Dark Felines in Unrest: Images of Political agitation**

Dark felines, frequently connected with strange notions, took on new imagery in progressive settings. This segment analyzes the utilization of dark felines as images of turmoil and defiance, especially in enemy of dictator developments.

VIII. Felines in Mainstream society and Marketing

1. **Felines as Social Symbols: Effect on Mainstream society**
   Felines play rose above their part as homegrown pets to become social symbols with a critical effect on workmanship, writing, and diversion. This part investigates how felines impact mainstream society and shape cultural discernments.

2. **The Promoting Blast: Commercialization of Feline Images**

The prominence of felines in friendly developments has converted into a flourishing business sector for feline related stock. This segment dives into the marketing peculiarity, investigating the commodification of feline images and its effect on buyer culture.

IX. Difficulties, Reactions, and Moral Contemplations

1. **Commercialization and Allocation: Difficult exercise**
   The utilization of felines as images in friendly developments has not been without challenges, including issues of commercialization and social allocation. This segment investigates occurrences where feline images have been co-selected benefit and the moral contemplations encompassing their utilization.
2. **Feline Government assistance: Moral Treatment in Activism**

As felines become images of social developments, concerns emerge with respect to their government assistance and moral treatment.

This part digs into the moral contemplations encompassing the utilization of felines in fights, workmanship, and online substance, tending to the harmony among imagery and creature government assistance.

X. Future Patterns and Developments

1. **Felines in Arising Social Developments**
   As friendly developments advance, felines keep on tracking down new jobs as images of opposition, activism, and social change. This part investigates expected patterns in the utilization of felines in arising social developments, from ecological activism to advanced privileges support.
2. **Molding the Story: Proceeded with Impact of Feline Culture**

The persevering through allure of felines as images recommends that their impact in forming cultural stories will endure. This part considers the proceeded with effect of feline culture on friendly developments and imagines how felines might assume a part in forming future stories of progress.

8.1 Cats in Political and Social Activism

Felines, with their smooth disposition and puzzling quality, have tracked down an unmistakable spot in our homes as well as in the powerful scene of political and social activism. This extensive investigation plans to dive into the multi-layered jobs that felines play in these circles. From emblematic portrayals to dynamic members, felines have woven their direction into the texture of activism, passing on messages of dissent, fortitude, and change.

B. The Puzzling Appeal of Felines in Activism

This part sets the stage by examining the exceptional allure of felines in activism. Their web popularity, verifiable imagery, and capacity to dazzle assorted crowds make them amazing assets for passing on messages and cultivating commitment in political and social causes.

II. Verifiable Imagery of Felines in Activism

1. **Old Egypt: Felines as Images of Security**

   In old Egypt, felines were worshipped and related with security and holiness. This part investigates the authentic imagery of felines in antiquated activism, taking into account their jobs as defenders and adored images.

2. **Archaic Europe: Felines as Focuses of Odd notion**

The Medieval times saw a change in discernment as felines, especially dark felines, became related with strange notions and black magic. This segment investigates how felines were focused on and oppressed during this period.

III. Felines in Political Kid's shows and Parody

1. **Felines as Political Images in Workmanship**

   Political kid's shows have a long history of utilizing creatures, including felines, as emblematic portrayals of political figures and philosophies. This part investigates the utilization of felines in political parody, dissecting their job in passing on complex political messages.

2. **Felines as Political Figures: Purposeful anecdotes and Exaggerations**

Since the beginning of time, felines have been represented as political figures in ironical outlines. This part digs into the figurative portrayals of felines as political pioneers, looking at the subtleties of these cartoons.

IV. Felines as Web Activists: Ascent of Feline Images

1. **The Introduction of Web Feline Images**
   The web time denoted another part in the job of felines in activism, with the ascent of images and viral substance. This part follows the introduction of web feline images, from early gatherings to the worldwide peculiarity they are today.

2. **Surly Feline and Viral Dispute**

Surly Feline, with her ceaselessly disappointed articulation, inadvertently turned into a symbol of contradiction and obstruction. This segment investigates the surprising ascent of Grouchy Feline and her effect on the crossing point of felines and virtual entertainment activism.

V. Felines in Civil rights Developments

1. **Women's liberation and Feline Imagery**
   Felines have shown up in women's activist developments, representing freedom, flexibility, and strengthening. This part investigates the presence of felines in women's activist iconography and their job in passing on messages of orientation fairness.

2. **Dark Felines in Progressive Symbolism**

Dark felines, frequently connected with strange notions, took on new imagery in progressive settings. This segment analyzes the utilization of dark felines as images of political agitation and disobedience, especially in enemy of dictator developments.

VI. VIP Felines and Social Activism

1. **Big name Felines as Diplomats**
   Web renowned felines like Lil Buddy and Colonel Yowl have

become envoys for social causes. This part investigates how big name felines influence their distinction to advance activism, bring issues to light, and add to beneficent endeavors.

2. **The Feline as an Image of Dissent**

Felines have become strong images of dissent, with their pictures highlighted on signs, standards, and virtual entertainment during different developments. This segment looks at how felines act as visual portrayals of difference and activism.

VII. Felines In broad daylight Fights and Showings

1. **Cat Members in Fights**
   Felines have been dynamic members out in the open fights, going to walks and exhibitions close by their human colleagues. This part investigates occurrences of felines joining activists in the city and the effect of their presence on the general population.

2. **Felines in Guerrilla Activism**

Guerrilla activism frequently includes startling and innovative strategies to pass on messages. This part dives into cases where felines have been utilized in guerrilla activism, from road craftsmanship to execution fights.

VIII. Felines and Advanced Activism

1. **#CatActivism: Felines via Virtual Entertainment Stages**
   Virtual entertainment stages have become landmarks for activism, and felines assume a critical part in computerized developments. This part investigates how hashtags like #CatActivism are utilized to bring issues to light, advance causes, and join feline sweethearts around friendly issues.

2. **Feline Powerhouses and Their Effect**

Feline powerhouses on stages like Instagram and TikTok employ impressive impact. This part analyzes how feline powerhouses influence their prominence to advocate for social and political causes, contacting assorted crowds with their messages.

IX. Difficulties, Reactions, and Moral Contemplations

1. **Commercialization and Assignment**
   The utilization of felines in activism raises moral contemplations, including occasions of commercialization and social allotment. This segment investigates situations where feline images have been co-selected benefit and the moral difficulties encompassing their utilization.
2. **Creature Government assistance in Activism**

As felines become images of political and social causes, concerns emerge with respect to their government assistance and moral treatment. This part dives into the moral contemplations encompassing the utilization of felines in fights, workmanship, and online substance, tending to the harmony among imagery and creature government assistance.

X. Felines in Worldwide Developments

1. **Worldwide Viewpoints: Felines in Worldwide Activism**
   Felines rise above social limits and have become images in worldwide developments. This segment investigates global viewpoints on felines in activism, analyzing how they are seen and used in various districts.
2. **Felines and Common freedoms Activism**

Felines have shown up in common liberties activism, representing opportunity and strength. This segment investigates examples where felines have become images of trust and fortitude despite common freedoms challenges.

XI. Future Patterns and Developments

1. **Felines in Arising Lobbyist Developments**
   As lobbyist developments develop, felines keep on tracking down new jobs as images of obstruction, support, and social change. This segment investigates expected patterns in the utilization of felines in arising dissident developments, from ecological activism to advanced privileges support.
2. **The Convergence of Feline Culture and Activism**

The getting through allure of felines as images proposes that their impact in molding cultural stories will continue. This segment ponders the proceeded with effect of feline culture on activism and imagines how felines might assume a part in molding future stories of progress.

8.2 Feline Symbols in Protests and Movements

1. **The Force of the Murmur: Felines as Images in Activism**
   Felines, with their elegance and baffling presence, have risen above the domain of friendship to become strong images in fights and social developments. This complete investigation digs into the complex jobs that catlike images play in activism, spreading over verifiable settings, web upsets, and worldwide developments. From old civic establishments to contemporary fights, felines have scratched their paw prints on the material of activism, passing on messages of opposition, fortitude, and cultural change.
2. **Cat Images Across Time and Societies**

This segment presents the getting through imagery of felines across different societies and time spans. From respected figures in old Egypt to current web images, felines have advanced as adaptable images with the capacity to reverberate with different crowds.

II. Authentic Cat Imagery

1. **Felines in Old Egypt: Gatekeepers and Heavenly Friends**
   Old Egypt loved felines, partner them with security and holiness.

This segment investigates the verifiable imagery of felines in old activism, featuring their jobs as watchmen and adored friends.

2. **Archaic Europe: Felines as Focuses of Strange notion**

The Medieval times saw a change in discernment as felines, especially dark felines, became related with strange notions and black magic. This segment looks at how felines were designated and mistreated during this period, differentiating their loved status in old Egypt.

III. Renaissance and Edification: Felines in Workmanship and Science

1. **Felines in Renaissance Craftsmanship: Images of Style and Secret**
   The Renaissance saw a resurgence of interest in felines, depicting them as images of tastefulness and secret in workmanship. This segment investigates the portrayal of felines in canvases and writing during this period.

2. **Edification Time: Felines and Logic**

The Edification got a shift mentalities towards creatures, and felines started to be viewed as animals deserving of logical request and perception. This segment looks at what the Illumination time meant for the impression of felines and their consideration in logical talk.

IV. Felines in Political Kid's shows and Parody

1. **Felines as Political Images in Workmanship**
   Political kid's shows have a rich history of utilizing creatures, including felines, as emblematic portrayals of political figures and philosophies. This part investigates the utilization of felines in political parody, breaking down their job in passing on complex political messages.

2. **Felines as Political Figures: Purposeful anecdotes and Personifications**

Since forever ago, felines have been embodied as political figures in humorous representations. This part dives into the symbolic portrayals of felines as political pioneers, analyzing the subtleties of these personifications.

V. Present day Cat Activism: Ascent of Feline Images

1. **The Introduction of Web Feline Images**
   The web period denoted a change in outlook in the job of felines as images in activism, with the ascent of images and viral substance. This segment follows the introduction of web feline images, from early gatherings to the worldwide peculiarity they are today.
2. **Cranky Feline and Viral Contradiction**

Testy Feline, with her never-endingly disappointed articulation, accidentally turned into a symbol of difference and obstruction. This segment investigates the surprising ascent of Testy Feline and her effect on the crossing point of felines and web-based entertainment activism.

VI. Felines in Civil rights Developments

1. **Woman's rights and Feline Imagery**
   Felines have shown up in women's activist developments, representing autonomy, strength, and strengthening. This segment investigates the presence of felines in women's activist iconography and their part in passing on messages of orientation balance.
2. **Dark Felines in Progressive Symbolism**

Dark felines, frequently connected with odd notions, took on new imagery in progressive settings. This segment analyzes the utilization of dark felines as images of disorder and disobedience, especially in enemy of dictator developments.

VII. Big name Felines and Social Activism

1. **Superstar Felines as Representatives**
   Web popular felines like Lil Pal and Colonel Yowl have become ministers for social causes. This segment investigates how superstar felines influence their popularity to advance activism, bring issues to light, and add to beneficent endeavors.
2. **The Feline as an Image of Dissent**

Felines have become strong images of dissent, with their pictures highlighted on signs, standards, and web-based entertainment during different developments. This segment inspects how felines act as visual portrayals of contradiction and activism.

VIII. Felines In broad daylight Fights and Shows

1. **Cat Members in Fights**
   Felines have been dynamic members openly dissents, going to walks and exhibitions close by their human friends. This part investigates cases of felines joining activists in the city and the effect of their presence on general society.
2. **Felines in Guerrilla Activism**

Guerrilla activism frequently includes unforeseen and imaginative strategies to pass on messages. This segment digs into examples where felines have been utilized in guerrilla activism, from road craftsmanship to execution fights.

IX. Felines and Advanced Activism

1. **#CatActivism: Felines via Online Entertainment Stages**
   Online entertainment stages have become landmarks for activism, and felines assume a huge part in computerized developments. This part investigates how hashtags like #CatActivism are utilized to bring issues to light, advance causes, and join feline darlings around friendly issues.
2. **Feline Powerhouses and Their Effect**

Feline powerhouses on stages like Instagram and TikTok use significant impact. This part looks at how feline powerhouses influence their prominence to advocate for social and political causes, contacting different crowds with their messages.

X. Difficulties, Reactions, and Moral Contemplations

1. **Commercialization and Apportionment**
   The utilization of felines in activism raises moral contemplations, including occasions of commercialization and social apportionment. This segment investigates situations where feline images have been co-decided on benefit and the moral problems encompassing their utilization.
2. **Creature Government assistance in Activism**

As felines become images of political and social causes, concerns emerge with respect to their government assistance and moral treatment. This part digs into the moral contemplations encompassing the utilization of felines in fights, craftsmanship, and online substance, tending to the harmony among imagery and creature government assistance.

XI. Felines in Worldwide Developments

1. **Worldwide Viewpoints: Felines in Worldwide Activism**
   Felines rise above social limits and have become images in worldwide developments. This segment investigates global points of view on felines in activism, analyzing how they are seen and used in various districts.
2. **Felines and Common liberties Activism**

Felines have shown up in basic liberties activism, representing opportunity and flexibility. This part investigates occurrences where felines have become images of trust and fortitude notwithstanding common freedoms challenges.

XII. Future Patterns and Developments

1. **Felines in Arising Lobbyist Developments**
   As lobbyist developments advance, felines keep on tracking down new jobs as images of opposition, support, and social change. This segment investigates expected patterns in the utilization of felines in arising lobbyist developments, from ecological activism to computerized freedoms promotion.
2. **The Convergence of Feline Culture and Activism**

The persevering through allure of felines as images proposes that their impact in forming cultural accounts will endure. This part ponders the proceeded with effect of feline culture on activism and imagines how felines might assume a part in molding future stories of progress.

8.3 Cats as Icons of Resistance and Resilience

1. **The Confounding Cat: From Allies to Symbols**
   Felines, with their smooth presence and free soul, play rose above their parts as simple allies to become strong images of opposition and versatility. This thorough investigation dives into the complex manners by which felines, over the entire course of time and across societies, have arisen as symbols addressing the getting through human soul against misfortune.
2. **Unwinding Cat Imagery**

This part presents the intrinsic imagery of felines, featuring their baffling nature, versatility, and verifiable importance. Felines, respected, dreaded, or revered, have woven themselves into the texture of human awareness, filling in as impressions of obstruction notwithstanding challenges.

II. Verifiable Points of view: Felines as Gatekeepers and Signs

1. **Old Egypt: Felines as Heavenly Defenders**
   In old Egypt, felines were respected as defenders, and the goddess Bastet exemplified their heavenly pith. This part investigates the

job of felines in old Egyptian culture, filling in as images of security and guardianship.

2. **Middle age Europe: Felines as Signs and Witches' Familiars**

The Medieval times got a shift insight, with felines, particularly dark felines, being related with strange notions and blamed for being witches' familiars. This segment dives into the dull periods of cat oppression and investigates how felines became the two signs and substitutes.

III. Renaissance to Edification: Felines in Workmanship and Illumination

1. **Renaissance Craftsmanship: Felines as Images of Class**
   The Renaissance saw a resurgence of interest in felines, depicting them as images of class and secret in craftsmanship. This part investigates the portrayal of felines in works of art and writing during this period.

2. **Edification Time: Felines and Realism**

The Edification time got a shift perspectives towards creatures, and felines started to be viewed as animals deserving of logical request and perception. This segment looks at what the Illumination meant for the view of felines and their consideration in logical talk.

IV. Felines in Political Kid's shows and Parody

1. **Felines as Political Images in Workmanship**
   Political kid's shows have a long history of utilizing creatures, including felines, as emblematic portrayals of political figures and philosophies. This part investigates the utilization of felines in political parody, examining their job in passing on complex political messages.

2. **Felines as Political Figures: Purposeful anecdotes and Cartoons**

Since forever ago, felines have been exemplified as political figures in sarcastic delineations. This part digs into the metaphorical portrayals of felines as political pioneers, inspecting the subtleties of these cartoons.

V. Present day Cat Activism: Ascent of Feline Images

1. **The Web Feline Upset**
   The coming of the web denoted another period for felines as images of opposition, with the ascent of images and viral substance. This part follows the introduction of web feline images, from early gatherings to the worldwide peculiarity they are today.
2. **Grouchy Feline and Viral Contradiction**

Grouchy Feline, with her interminably disappointed articulation, inadvertently turned into a symbol of contradiction and opposition. This part investigates the surprising ascent of Cranky Feline and her effect on the crossing point of felines and virtual entertainment activism.

VI. Felines in Civil rights Developments

1. **Woman's rights and Feline Imagery**
   Felines have shown up in women's activist developments, representing autonomy, flexibility, and strengthening. This segment investigates the presence of felines in women's activist iconography and their job in passing on messages of orientation uniformity.
2. **Dark Felines in Progressive Symbolism**

Dark felines, frequently connected with odd notions, took on new imagery in progressive settings. This segment analyzes the utilization of dark felines as images of political agitation and resistance, especially in enemy of tyrant developments.

VII. Big name Felines and Social Activism

1. **Big name Felines as Representatives**
   Web renowned felines like Lil Pal and Colonel Yowl have become

diplomats for social causes. This segment investigates how VIP felines influence their popularity to advance activism, bring issues to light, and add to altruistic endeavors.

2. The Feline as an Image of Dissent

Felines have become strong images of dissent, with their pictures included on signs, flags, and web-based entertainment during different developments. This part inspects how felines act as visual portrayals of contradiction and activism.

VIII. Felines Openly Fights and Exhibitions

1. Cat Members in Fights

Felines have been dynamic members openly dissents, going to walks and exhibitions close by their human partners. This segment investigates examples of felines joining activists in the city and the effect of their presence on people in general.

2. Felines in Guerrilla Activism

Guerrilla activism frequently includes surprising and imaginative strategies to pass on messages. This part dives into examples where felines have been utilized in guerrilla activism, from road workmanship to execution fights.

IX. Felines and Computerized Activism

1. #CatActivism: Felines via Virtual Entertainment Stages

Virtual entertainment stages have become milestones for activism, and felines assume a critical part in computerized developments. This segment investigates how hashtags like #CatActivism are utilized to bring issues to light, advance causes, and join feline sweethearts around friendly issues.

2. Feline Powerhouses and Their Effect

Feline powerhouses on stages like Instagram and TikTok employ significant impact. This part looks at how feline powerhouses influence their prominence to advocate for social and political causes, contacting different crowds with their messages.

X. Difficulties, Reactions, and Moral Contemplations

1. Commercialization and Apportionment

The utilization of felines in activism raises moral contemplations, including cases of commercialization and social appointment. This part investigates situations where feline images have been co-selected benefit and the moral problems encompassing their utilization.

2. Creature Government assistance in Activism

As felines become images of political and social causes, concerns emerge in regards to their government assistance and moral treatment. This segment dives into the moral contemplations encompassing the utilization of felines in fights, craftsmanship, and online substance, tending to the harmony among imagery and creature government assistance.

XI. Felines in Worldwide Developments

1. Worldwide Viewpoints: Felines in Worldwide Activism

Felines rise above social limits and have become images in worldwide developments. This part investigates global viewpoints on felines in activism, looking at how they are seen and used in various locales.

2. Felines and Common freedoms Activism

Felines have shown up in common liberties activism, representing opportunity and flexibility. This segment investigates occurrences where felines have become images of trust and fortitude despite basic freedoms challenges.

XII. Future Patterns and Advancements

1. **Felines in Arising Lobbyist Developments**
   As lobbyist developments advance, felines keep on tracking down new jobs as images of opposition, backing, and social change. This segment investigates possible patterns in the utilization of felines in arising extremist developments, from natural activism to computerized freedoms promotion.
2. **The Convergence of Feline Culture and Activism**

The getting through allure of felines as images recommends that their impact in molding cultural stories will persevere. This part ponders the proceeded with effect of feline culture on activism and imagines how felines might assume a part in forming future stories of progress.

Chapter 9

Cat Psychology And Pop Culture

Felines have been a piece of mankind's set of experiences for millennia, loved in old societies and esteemed as darling buddies in current times. The remarkable brain research of felines has entranced people for ages, and as of late, their way of behaving has become interlaced with mainstream society. This paper investigates the perplexing universe of feline brain science, digging into the intricacies of cat conduct and analyzing how these baffling animals have become conspicuous figures in the domain of mainstream society.

1. **The Development of Felines and Their Taming:**
   To comprehend feline brain science, it is fundamental to dive into the transformative history of these animals. Wildcats, Felis silvestris lybica, are accepted to be the progenitors of the cutting edge homegrown feline, Felis catus. Felines started their excursion close by people as nuisance regulators, progressively acquiring their keep and becoming colleagues. The training system was one of a kind, as felines held their freedom and numerous wild senses. Felines show a scope of ways of behaving established in their

developmental past. Hunting, regional checking, preparing, and correspondence through non-verbal communication are fundamental parts of cat conduct. Understanding these ways of behaving is pivotal for feline proprietors and devotees to cultivate positive associations with their catlike sidekicks.

2. **The Mysterious Idea of Feline Way of behaving:**

Not at all like canines, which have been specifically reproduced for different undertakings and show more unmistakable social ways of behaving, felines hold a level of ferocity. Their way of behaving can be perplexing, frequently trying for people to decipher. The apparently reserved nature of felines is a typical generalization, yet it originates from their developmental history as lone trackers.

Felines impart utilizing an unpretentious language that incorporates body developments, vocalizations, and fragrance checking. Understanding these prompts permits feline proprietors to unravel their pets' feelings and necessities. Murmuring, for instance, can flag happiness, while murmuring might demonstrate dread or hostility. By perceiving these prompts, proprietors can establish conditions that take care of their felines' regular impulses.

3. **Feline Conduct in the Home Climate:**

Felines are regional animals, and their conduct inside the house is much of the time affected by their need to lay out and keep up with an area. Scratching, for example, fills the double need of checking an area and keeping up with solid hooks. Giving felines fitting scratching posts can divert this conduct in a positive manner.

The presentation of new pets or changes in the family can influence a feline's way of behaving, at times prompting pressure related issues. Figuring out the indications of stress, like unreasonable preparing or stowing away, permits proprietors to speedily resolve these issues. Establishing an invigorating climate with toys, climbing structures, and intelligent play can add to a feline's psychological and actual prosperity.

4. **Felines in Mainstream society:**

Felines have penetrated mainstream society in different structures, becoming notable figures in writing, craftsmanship, and media. From old Egyptian folklore, where felines were related with the goddess Bastet, to the Cheshire Feline in Lewis Carroll's "Alice's Experiences in Wonderland," cats have held a unique spot in the human creative mind.

In the domain of film and TV, felines have been highlighted in various jobs, going from energized characters like Tom in "Tom and Jerry" to the superb depiction of the Choupette feline in design symbol Karl Lagerfeld's life. The web, with its huge swath of feline images, recordings, and virtual entertainment accounts, has moved felines to fame, transforming them into web sensations.

5. **Web Feline Culture and the Ascent of "Catfluencers":**

The coming of the web and virtual entertainment stages has led to a peculiarity known as "catfluencers" - felines with enormous internet based followings. Irritable Feline, Lil Buddy, and Nala Feline are only a couple of instances of cat VIPs that have caught the hearts of millions. The allure of web feline culture lies in the humor, charm, and appeal of felines' ways of behaving.

Feline recordings and images overwhelm stages like YouTube, Instagram, and TikTok. The prominence of these web-based cat VIPs has engaged as well as set out open doors for brand organizations, product, and, surprisingly, generous undertakings. The progress of web feline culture features society's interest with these secretive yet charming animals.

6. **Feline Brain science in the Time of Innovation:**

Innovation plays had a critical impact in understanding and taking special care of the mental necessities of felines. Intelligent toys, robotized feeders, and, surprisingly, computer generated reality encounters for felines have arisen as instruments to advance their current circumstance.

Understanding the effect of screen time on felines' emotional wellness is a continuous area of examination, as additional proprietors integrate advanced diversion into their pets' lives.

Virtual feline games and recordings intended to draw in and engage felines have become famous. These advanced encounters expect to take advantage of felines' hunting senses, giving mental feeling in an indoor setting. Be that as it may, it is fundamental for feline proprietors to offset computerized communication with genuine encounters to guarantee a comprehensive way to deal with their pets' prosperity.

7. **Feline Way of behaving and Human Prosperity:**

The constructive outcomes of feline proprietorship on human prosperity are irrefutably factual. The friendship, stress alleviation, and satisfaction that felines bring to their proprietors add to in general mental and profound wellbeing. Studies have shown that cooperating with felines can bring down circulatory strain, diminish tension, and ease sensations of depression.

Treatment felines, prepared to give solace and backing in different settings, have become basic to psychological well-being drives. The non-critical nature of felines and their natural comprehension of human feelings make them ideal allies for those out of luck. Subsequently, felines play tracked down parts in medical services offices, schools, and even catastrophe reaction groups, giving comfort in the midst of pain.

8. **Moral Contemplations in Feline Proprietorship and Media Abuse:**

While the coordination of felines into mainstream society and media has given pleasure to many, it is vital for address moral contemplations encompassing the utilization of felines for diversion purposes. The government assistance of VIP felines, particularly those with broad internet based followings, should be vital. Capable proprietorship, legitimate veterinary consideration, and contemplations for a feline's prosperity ought not be compromised for web popularity.

The peculiarity of "duping" - making counterfeit records or personas for felines on the web - brings up issues about the limits between innocuous tomfoolery and possible double-dealing. The moral utilization of felines in media includes regarding their independence, guaranteeing their physical and mental prosperity, and taking into account their regular ways of behaving in any type of diversion.

9.1 The Therapeutic Power of Cats

Felines, with their perplexing characters and mitigating presence, have for quite some time been perceived for their restorative advantages. Past the domain of simple friendship, felines play played crucial parts in the close to home, mental, and actual prosperity of people.

This article dives into the multi-layered remedial force of felines, investigating the manners by which cat friendship emphatically influences human wellbeing, from lessening pressure and nervousness to supporting the therapy of different ailments.

1. **The Mending Contact: Profound Prosperity and Stress Decrease**

1. **Friendship and Solace:**
   The simple presence of a feline can give a feeling of solace and friendship that is unrivaled. The cadenced murmuring of a substance feline has been logically connected to pressure decrease. Murmuring isn't just an indication of unwinding for the feline yet additionally a wellspring of comfort for people. The low-recurrence vibrations created during murmuring have been related with the arrival of endorphins, the body's normal warm hearted synthetic substances, advancing a feeling of quiet and prosperity.

2. **Stress and Nervousness Decrease:**

Various examinations have exhibited the pressure lessening impacts of connecting with felines. The demonstration of petting a feline triggers the arrival of oxytocin, frequently alluded to as the "adoration chemical" or "holding chemical." Oxytocin is known to lessen pressure and uneasiness levels, advancing a feeling of trust and close to home association. For people managing regular stressors or adapting to emotional well-being conditions, the quieting impact of a feline can be an important wellspring of help.

II. Felines as Basic encouragement Creatures:

1. **Lawful Acknowledgment and Advantages:**
   Felines, alongside canines, have earned respect as daily reassurance creatures (ESAs) in numerous locales. Daily reassurance creatures give friendship and solace to people managing emotional well-being conditions like nervousness, despondency, or post-horrendous pressure problem (PTSD). The lawful assignment of felines as ESAs permits people to profit from their remedial presence in different settings, including lodging and travel.

2. **Holding and Association:**

The connection between a feline and its proprietor can be significant, making a feeling of profound security and steadiness. Felines are natural creatures, frequently detecting changes feeling their proprietors' or personal states. This instinctive association can be especially significant for people confronting inner difficulties, giving a non-critical wellspring of help and friendship.

III. Actual Medical advantages of Feline Friendship:

1. **Cardiovascular Wellbeing:**
   Research proposes that claiming a feline can decidedly affect cardiovascular wellbeing. The quieting presence of a feline, joined with the demonstration of petting, has been related with lower circulatory strain and pulse. These physiological changes add to

by and large cardiovascular prosperity, diminishing the gamble of heart-related conditions.

2. **Actual work and Exercise:**

While felines are frequently connected with relaxing and snoozing, they additionally energize actual work in their proprietors. Intelligent play with felines, including toys and exercises that copy hunting ways of behaving, gives a great way to people to remain dynamic. The actual commitment expected for play helps the feline as well as advances practice for the proprietor, adding to a better way of life.

IV. Felines in Restorative Settings:

1. **Creature Helped Treatment:**
   Creature helped treatment (AAT) includes the consideration of creatures, including felines, in remedial mediations to upgrade physical, close to home, and social prosperity. In clinical settings, prepared treatment felines work close by medical services experts to help people managing a scope of conditions, from uneasiness and misery to formative problems.

2. **Remedial Appearance Projects:**

Restorative appearance programs bring prepared treatment felines into different settings, including medical clinics, nursing homes, and schools. These projects plan to give solace, friendship, and basic reassurance to people confronting wellbeing challenges. The presence of a treatment feline has been displayed to mitigate pressure, diminish nervousness, and work on the general state of mind of those getting care.

V. Felines and Adapting to Injury:

1. **Injury Informed Care:**
   Felines can assume an essential part in injury informed care, giving a safe and harmless presence for people who have encountered injury. The delicate, non-requesting nature of felines permits

injury survivors to lay out a feeling of control and wellbeing in their current circumstance. The method involved with really focusing on a feline can likewise encourage a feeling of obligation and strengthening for people on their recuperating venture.

2. **PTSD and Backing:**

For people adapting to post-horrendous pressure issue (PTSD), felines can offer significant help. The quieting impacts of cat friendship can assist with relieving side effects like hypervigilance and tension. Moreover, the daily practice and design engaged with really focusing on a feline can add to a feeling of security for those exploring the difficulties of PTSD.

VI. Felines in Hospice and Palliative Consideration:

1. **End-of-Life Friendship:**
   Felines have a special capacity to give solace and friendship during end-of-life care. In hospice and palliative consideration settings, treatment felines offer comfort to people confronting terminal ailments. The delicate presence of a feline can give snapshots of pleasure and association, establishing a calming climate for the two patients and their friends and family.

2. **Loss Backing:**

After the departure of a friend or family member, felines can assume a critical part in giving deprivation support. The genuine love and calm friendship they proposition can be particularly ameliorating during seasons of melancholy. The daily practice and care engaged with taking care of a feline can likewise give a feeling of inspiration to people exploring the difficulties of misfortune.

VII. Difficulties and Obligations of Feline Proprietorship in Treatment:

1. **Sensitivities and Awarenesses:**
   While the remedial advantages of feline friendship are huge, recognizing potential challenges is fundamental. Aversions to feline dander can present wellbeing takes a chance for certain people, restricting the possibility of feline possession in specific settings. In remedial conditions, cautious thought of sensitivities and awarenesses is vital to guarantee the prosperity of the two clients and guardians.

2. **Moral Contemplations:**

The utilization of felines in treatment raises moral contemplations with respect to their prosperity and solace. Treatment felines should go through legitimate preparation to guarantee they are agreeable and composed in helpful settings. Moreover, moral contemplations reach out to the expected abuse of treatment creatures, underscoring the significance of dependable proprietorship and treatment.

9.2 Emotional Support Animals and Therapy Cats

The utilization of creatures for helpful purposes has earned extensive respect lately, with everyday encouragement creatures (ESAs) and treatment felines arising as significant sidekicks in advancing emotional well-being and prosperity. This paper investigates the significant effect of everyday encouragement creatures and treatment felines on people battling with psychological well-being difficulties, digging into the restorative advantages, moral contemplations, and the job these creatures play in upgrading the general personal satisfaction for their human sidekicks.

1. **Figuring out Basic encouragement Creatures (ESAs):**
1. **Lawful Acknowledgment and Definition:**
   Daily reassurance creatures are buddy creatures that give solace, friendship, and basic encouragement to people managing emotional well-being conditions. Not at all like help creatures, which are prepared to perform explicit undertakings for people with

handicaps, ESAs don't go through specific preparation. Nonetheless, they are safeguarded under the law in specific locales, conceding people the option to have their basic encouragement creatures with them in different settings, including lodging and air travel.

2. **Remedial Advantages of ESAs:**

The essential remedial advantage of everyday reassurance creatures lies in their capacity to give close to home solace and strength. The genuine love and friendship presented by ESAs can fundamentally lessen side effects of tension, wretchedness, and other psychological well-being problems. The presence of an ESA frequently assists people with feeling more grounded and upheld, cultivating a feeling of association and reason.

II. The Job of Felines as Basic encouragement Creatures:

1. **Exceptional Characteristics of Felines as ESAs:**
While canines are all the more generally connected with everyday reassurance jobs, felines have special characteristics that make them appropriate for this reason. The quieting impact of a murmuring feline, the delicate friendship they give, and their natural comprehension of human feelings make them ideal consistent reassurance creatures for people who might favor a more free or low-support sidekick.
2. **Advantages of Feline Friendship for Emotional wellness:**

Stress Decrease: The demonstration of petting a feline has been displayed to bring down feelings of anxiety and advance unwinding. The cadenced murmuring of a substance feline has a quieting impact, delivering endorphins and decreasing cortisol, the pressure chemical.

Reducing Depression: Felines, with their friendly nature, offer friendship and lighten sensations of forlornness. The everyday practice of really focusing on a feline gives design and motivation, especially useful for people managing seclusion or burdensome side effects.

Non-Critical Friendship: Felines are non-critical and tolerating, making a place of refuge for people to communicate their feelings unafraid of analysis. This unqualified acknowledgment is essential for those exploring the difficulties of emotional wellness conditions.

III. Treatment Felines: Improving Mental Prosperity through Connection

1. **Definition and Preparing of Treatment Felines:**
   Treatment felines are explicitly prepared creatures that work in different remedial settings to offer close to home help, solace, and friendship. Not at all like help creatures with legitimate access freedoms, treatment felines frequently work in medical care offices, schools, and different foundations where their quieting presence can help people confronting physical or psychological wellness challenges.

2. **Remedial Advantages of Interfacing with Treatment Felines:**

Stress Decrease and Unwinding: The presence of a treatment feline has been connected to pressure decrease and unwinding. Connecting with a quiet and thoroughly prepared feline can establish a relieving climate, assisting people with overseeing tension and feelings of anxiety.

Improved Temperament and Prosperity: The positive effect of treatment felines on state of mind is apparent in different restorative settings. Whether visiting patients in medical clinics or offering help to people in nursing homes, treatment felines add to worked on profound prosperity.

Social Connection and Correspondence: Treatment felines work with social association and correspondence, especially in populaces where verbal correspondence might challenge. The non-verbal and harmless nature of felines urges people to communicate their thoughts and participate in significant associations.

IV. Moral Contemplations in the Utilization of Treatment Felines:

1. **Government assistance and Prosperity of Treatment Felines:**
   The moral utilization of treatment felines requires cautious thought of their government assistance and prosperity. Treatment felines ought to go through legitimate preparation to guarantee they are agreeable and versatile to different conditions.
   Normal veterinary consideration, proper rest periods, and observing of feelings of anxiety are fundamental parts of mindful possession in treatment feline projects.
2. **Assent and Limits:**

Regarding the assent and limits of people in helpful settings is fundamental. While many individuals find solace within the sight of treatment felines, it is urgent to guarantee that those getting care are familiar with and agree to the association. Clear correspondence and aversion to individual necessities add to a positive and moral remedial experience.

V. Legitimate Contemplations and Difficulties:

1. **Legitimate Assurances for Treatment Felines:**
   Treatment felines don't have similar legitimate insurances as administration creatures, which are prepared to perform explicit undertakings for people with incapacities. The presence of treatment felines openly spaces is many times subject to the arrangements of the particular foundation or office where they are working. Clear correspondence and joint effort with medical care experts, teachers, and office managers are fundamental to explore lawful contemplations.
2. **Public Discernment and Disgrace:**

Regardless of the helpful advantages they offer, treatment felines might confront difficulties connected with public discernment and shame. Misinterpretations about the job and viability of treatment creatures can add to doubt or obstruction in specific conditions. Instruction and mindfulness missions can assist with scattering legends and advance a superior comprehension of the positive effect treatment felines can have on mental prosperity.

VI. The Eventual fate of Everyday encouragement Creatures and Treatment Felines:

1. **Exploration and Progressions:**
   Proceeded with examination into the remedial advantages of basic reassurance creatures and treatment felines is fundamental for extending how we might interpret their effect on emotional well-being. Headways in preparing methods, creature helped mediations, and the mix of innovation might additionally upgrade the viability of these mediations in different remedial settings.
2. **Psychological wellness Backing and Reconciliation:**

As the acknowledgment of psychological well-being difficulties develops, there is a rising requirement for psychological well-being backing and the reconciliation of steady intercessions.

Daily reassurance creatures and treatment felines can assume vital parts in all encompassing psychological wellness care, supplementing conventional remedial methodologies and giving remarkable roads to everyday encouragement and association.

9.3 Cats in Pop Culture Psychology

Felines have instilled themselves into the woven artwork of human culture, turning out to be something other than pets. Their baffling appeal, free nature, and particular ways of behaving have made them notable figures in mainstream society. This exposition investigates the convergence of felines in mainstream society and brain science, diving into the manners by which these cryptic cats enthrall our minds, shape our discernments, and reflect parts of human brain science.

1. **Old Images to Present day Symbols: Felines in Folklore and Old stories**
1. **Old Egypt and the Goddess Bastet:**
   Felines have a rich history saturated with folklore, with maybe the most prominent affiliation being with the old Egyptians. Felines were loved and connected with the goddess Bastet, a divinity addressing home, fruitfulness, and security. Old Egyptians accepted that felines had defensive characteristics and brought favorable luck, prompting their boundless taming.
2. **Fables and Strange notions:**

Felines have additionally been unmistakable in different fables all over the planet, frequently exemplifying both positive and negative imagery. In certain societies, dark felines are viewed as carriers of best of luck, while in others, they are related with odd notions and black magic. This duality in social discernments mirrors the mind boggling and puzzling nature ascribed to felines since forever ago.

II. Felines in Writing and Workmanship: From Cheshire to Cranky

1. **Lewis Carroll's Cheshire Feline:**
   Lewis Carroll's "Alice's Undertakings in Wonderland" presented the notable Cheshire Feline, a smiling cat with the capacity to show up and vanish freely. The Cheshire Feline addresses caprice and conundrum, having an enduring impact on perusers and adding to the feline's persevering through fame in writing.
2. **Web Feline Sensations:**

In the computerized age, felines play taken on new parts as web sensations. Images, viral recordings, and online entertainment accounts devoted to felines have changed standard cats into VIPs. Cranky Feline, with her never-endingly disappointed articulation, and Lil Pal, with her one of a kind appearance and inspiring story, became web sensations, exhibiting the web's interest with felines.

III. Feline Recordings and the Force of Murmur suasion

1. **The Ascent of Feline Recordings:**
   The web is flooded with feline recordings that accumulate a huge number of perspectives, likes, and offers. The allure of these recordings lies in the humor, charm, and appeal of felines' ways of behaving. From perky shenanigans to charming ungainliness, feline recordings offer a wellspring of diversion that rises above social and phonetic limits.

2. **The Brain science of Feline Recordings:**

Mentally, feline recordings tap into different parts of human inclination and cognizance. Seeing a charming little cat can set off the arrival of oxytocin, the "adoration chemical," advancing good sentiments and holding. Moreover, the eccentricism and suddenness of felines' activities in recordings make a feeling of curiosity, keeping watchers drew in and engaged.

IV. Humanoid attribution: Extending Human Characteristics onto Cat Companions

1. **Adapting Felines in Media:**
   Humanoid attribution, the attribution of human qualities to non-human substances, is a pervasive subject in mainstream society highlighting felines. From vivified characters with human-like articulations to talking felines in writing and film, refining felines permits crowds to interface with these creatures on a more engaging level.

2. **The Effect on Insight:**

The inclination to humanize felines can impact how we see and associate with them. By ascribing human feelings and expectations to felines, we might shape more grounded profound bonds with our cat-like mates. Notwithstanding, it is crucial for offset humanoid attribution with a comprehension of felines' exceptional ways of behaving and correspondence styles.

V. Feline Bistros and Restorative Advantages

1. **The Worldwide Peculiarity of Feline Bistros:**
   Feline bistros, foundations that permit supporters to partake in the organization of occupant felines while tasting on espresso or tea, have turned into a worldwide peculiarity. Beginning in Taiwan, these bistros offer a special mix of unwinding and friendship, permitting guests to encounter the helpful advantages of cooperating with felines.

2. **The Restorative Force of Feline Bistros:**

Feline bistros give a quieting climate where supporters can de-stress and loosen up within the sight of felines. The demonstration of petting a feline has been connected to pressure decrease and the arrival of endorphins. Feline bistros offer a space for social collaboration and unwinding, overcoming any barrier between the restorative advantages of human-creature communication and the bistro culture.

VI. Feline Product and Buyer Brain research

1. **From Shirts to Toys: The Feline Product Blast:**
   The ubiquity of felines in mainstream society has led to a thriving business sector for feline themed stock. From dress and assistants to home stylistic layout and toys, feline themed items take special care of a different crowd of feline darlings. The allure of these things reaches out past utilitarian use, taking advantage of the profound association individuals have with felines.

2. **Close to home Marking and Buyer Conduct:**

Feline product frequently depends on close to home marking methodologies, utilizing the positive affiliations individuals have with felines to make an association between the customer and the item. The close to home allure of felines can impact shopper conduct, driving buys in view of a longing to communicate love for these creatures or offer in the delight they bring.

Paws and Icons: The Cultural Impact of Famous Cats - Solomon Raj

The "feline woman" generalization, frequently depicted in media as an offbeat and lone lady encompassed by various felines, has pervaded cultural discernments. While it is frequently utilized hilariously, the generalization can sustain negative suppositions about people who have cozy associations with felines, adding to social disgrace.

B. Real factors of Feline Friendship:

In actuality, individuals of all sexual orientations and ages structure profound associations with felines. The generalization disregards the positive parts of feline friendship, like the remedial advantages, everyday reassurance, and the delight that felines bring to the existences of their human sidekicks. Testing the feline woman generalization requires a change in cultural discernments and an appreciation for the different ways individuals experience cat friendship.

* 9 7 8 8 1 9 6 7 9 9 3 6 6 *